FAITH

Faith grows through listening to Neter and seeing the
results. In the summer of 2016, I was asked, "who do you work
for?" The answer I gave was not of me but of the I AM within.
I never shared or thought about the answer I provided.
Who do you work for, I was asked.
I stated with authority the answer,
"I work for the KINGDOM."
It was the most beautiful ah-ha moment in my world.
I knew it came from the Supreme Being.

~ Queen Phyllis L-Miata

I AM QUEEN MIATA (I AM MA'AT)

*I was given my Spiritual name, 'L', which sym-
bolizes Love, Life, and Light in 2016.*

*When Spirit gave me the name Miata on
April 30, 2017, Spirit told me it was the name
I am known by each time I incarnate. At that
time, I had no remembrance of the Energy of
Ma'at or my past lives. I only know to live
in the Knowing, in the trusting and listening to
the Creator.*

~ Queen Phyllis L-Miata

Your Greatest Potential, Your Household DNA, Your *I AM SPIRIT*

by *Queen Phyllis L-Miata*

PERSONAL MESSAGE

The process of writing this book took me to an amazing elevated level of Spiritual submissiveness and openness where I was so entranced in a cocoon of enlightenment and wisdom transforming me and ascending my soul.

I am humbled and honored by the message Spirit entrusted me to write. The message is awesome, enlightening and inspiring.

Enjoy, Rise, and Live in your Greatness.

~ Queen Phyllis L-Miata

***The Role of a Queen is in the Renewal and
Rebirth of the Fundamental Spirit
of a Culture, its Light.***

*Breathe, You are SPIRIT
Create, You are LIGHT
Transform, You are LOVE*

Permission To Be Great
3rd edition
Copyright ©2016, 2017, 2020 by Phyllis Austin, L-Miata

Phyllis L-Miata
2107 N. Decatur Rd. Suite 110
Decatur, GA 30033

Illustrator (Cover): Okomota

Library of Congress Catalog Control Number: 2017900110

ISBN 978-0-9759917-4-9

Printed in the United States of America

This book is for informational purposes only. Neither the author nor publisher assumes any responsibility for the use or misuse of information and sources contained in this book.

Contact Author:
Email: QueenMiata@OneNationEnlightened.net

Additional books can be ordered online at
www.OneNationEnlightened.net
www.PhyllisL-Miata.com

Contributing to the
Queen Phyllis L-Miata
Legacy

Dedications:

To my mother, Gazella Cooper, I honor her for instilling in me
the only boundaries on me are those that I place on myself.

To my father, Rev. George Cooper, I honor him for showing me
entrepreneurship.

To my children, Che'Malcolm and NiaImani, I honor them for
their energy, unconditional love, and support.

Acknowledgments:

First and foremost, I give NETER the glory for
grace, love and vision.

I thank a host of family, friends, colleagues, and associates
in the manifestation of this vision.

A special thanks to the Spirit of Joseph, Kirt Joseph,
for being a guiding light on my journey's path.

CONTENTS

Map of Nile River

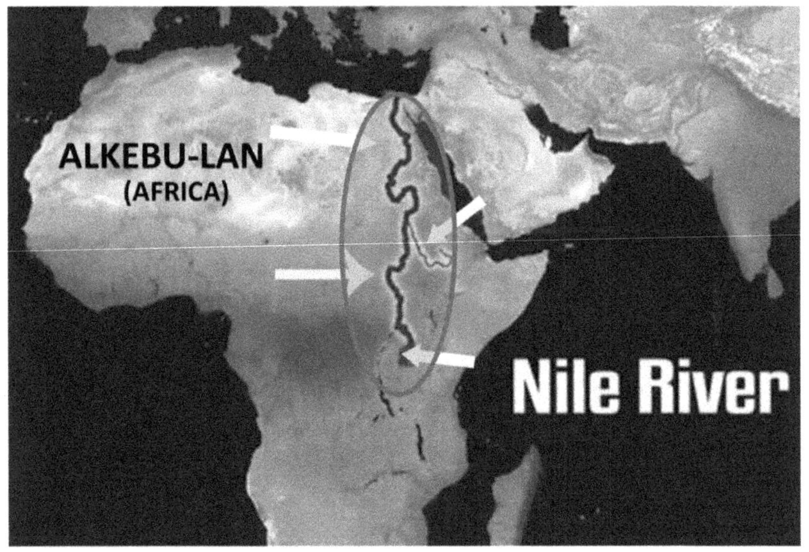

Map: Location of Ancient Kemet and Kush/Cush relative to today's African Countries

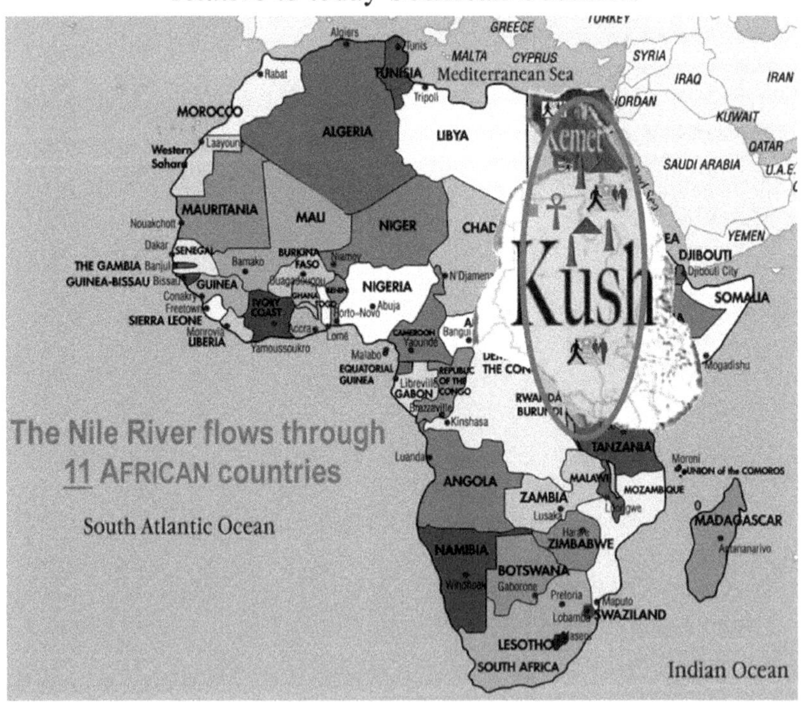

Introduction

Welcome to *Permission To Be Great*, which is part of
Queen Phyllis L-Miata's *Project L's Love, Life,* and *Light* series.

There is a Supreme of you within, consisting of magnificent creative energy and power. It is yours to access; it is your greatest potential; it is your transformative power to use and to elevate you and your household to Greatness.

This is *Permission To Be Great*: Your Greatest Potential, Your Household DNA, Your 'I AM SPIRIT'.

↔

As I engage in this Journey of Spiritual Enlightenment and Elevation, I have learned that the Spirit within will guide you to the truth of who you are. You only have to let Neter guide you, which means a willingness to go where the Divine Force leads you.

Irrespective of the term used (Enlightenment, Elevation, Ascension, etc), Neter leads one into the truth of one's Spiritual Self.

I want to share a story with you.

> *I overheard the conversation between three middle
> school-aged boys. Two of the boys, one identified
> himself as Black, and the other identified himself as
> White, were questioning the "race" of another student.
> I put quotations around the term race because race is a
> human term, not a Spiritual term.*

The 3rd boy was asked by the two boys, "are you Black or White?". The boy turned and firmly stated, "I am Italian." I thought to myself, someone taught him correctly. This boy knew his history was in Italy, not in America.

Chem and Khem mean Black, and Kemet means the '*Land of the Black*'. Therefore, if you identify yourself as Black, there is a history of you in Kemet. To fully understand the nature of your Spiritual existence, you must understand the history of Black people in Kemet and Civilizations along the Nile Valley River corridor.

↔

Since the original publication of this book, I have learned the following about the Stolen Legacy of Black people pertaining to the terms used in this book:

Upon the conquering of KEMET by the Greeks in 332 BC:

1) KEMET (KMT) was changed to Egypt (Greek word).
Please reference map on page 10.

2) GOD, a Greek word meaning power replaced the Kemetic word NETER (NTR), meaning NATURE.

Neter: The Ancestors' higher understanding of Creation
In Nature there is Divinity, a Divine Force that exists in all things created by the Divine Force, which is an Energy of Light that can produce itself and is able to create what we know as Life. Therefore, within Life is Light, a Divine Force (Divinity) that is constantly present, constantly creating, and constantly enlightening, an adaptive Life-force that will always lead Life back to its fundamental principle of Light.

Neter is Divine; it is the Divine referencing the Divinity of Nature and its Divine Force. When 't' is underlined, the sound is 'tch' and Ntr is pronounced Netcher. Neter expresses the noun and verb of the Creator. The term God denotes more of the noun of the Creator. Reference video NTR v. God at ***https://youtu.be/RmKRZJxOmEg*** and ***https://onenationenlightened.net/GlobalTV/on-demand/global-kingdom-message/***

Our Ancestors' language, civilizations, and creations demonstrated an understanding of the vastness of the Universe and the Neter (Divine Force) within Nature. Our Ancestors used different names for various aspects of Neter/Nature, recognizing the tangible and abstract characteristics of the Creator's creations and their elicited enlightenment.

(This practice of reverence for the Creator's creations has been misinterpreted as polytheism in translation.)

3) In Greek, 'THE ALL' and the 7 Universal Laws expressed in the Kybalion were copied/stolen from the concepts of Alkebu-Lan (Ancient Africa) civilizations and their inscriptions and the Kemites/Kemetic teachings including but not limited to: THE NETCHERU, Kemetic 7 Universal Laws teachings, the Medu Neter, and the Pert Em Heru n Gerh (The Book of Coming into the Light from Darkness) misnomer Egyptian Book of the Dead.

a. **THE NETCHERU** represents the Divine Universal Laws and Principles of and in Creation/Universe/Nature. The Neter is a sub-entity of the Divine Universal Laws and Principles present in creations.

Therefore, being made in the image and likeness of the Creator means one is made in and of the Divine Universal Laws and Principles, and one is/has the Neter (the Divine Force) within. The Divine Universal Laws and Principles govern the Divine Force.

Neter means Divine, Divinity, the Divine Creator, and the Divine Force within, which is Divine. Neter is what is.   Neter is Divinity in itself, and incorporated in the understanding of the Divine Force is *I AM that I AM.*

b. **The Pert Em Heru n Gerh misnomer Egyptian Book of the Dead:** "Pert," going out; "Em," as or through; "Heru," Spiritual Light or Enlightened Being (the Heru, the Light); Nehast, resurrect -wake up; and "Gerh", "Darkness". In short, Pert Em Heru means "Coming into the Light."

(According to cross-references, The Pert Em Heru originated from Alkebu-Lan pre-dynastic and dynastic civilizations' tomb paintings and inscriptions originating before 4000 BCE).

4) The Original Immaculate Conception story is of Ausar, Auset, and Heru. The Greeks copied the story using Osiris, Isis, and Horus respectively.

5) The MR (Mir) was changed to Pyramid, a Greek word. The Apex of the MR means ASCENSION, which affirms the importance of the structure.

6) The Medu Neter (Mdu Ntr) was changed to hieroglyphics, a Greek term.

7) Spirit is derived from the Latin word Spirae and Spiri, which means to breathe., i.e. respiration, is the act of breathing.

However, in various translations of the Medu Neter, **Soul** not Spirit is referenced. The Soul being the ***Life-Force,*** the ***Energy of Life***, the ***Living Energy*** that awakens self.

Here we have Soul being more of a noun-verb. When one breathes in the Life-Force / Living Energy, Man becomes a Living Soul (Life-Force) in alignment with the Neteru (Divine Consciousness/ Universe) being of / having the Neter (Divine Force) within.

Today's use of the term Spirit, in concept and context, is based on the meaning of Soul. In essence, the Breath of Life is the Spirit of Life, which is literally, The Soul of Life.

Other:
According to Anthony Browder's research, the Greeks referenced Imhotep as the Christ.

(Just a reminder that Christ, a Greek word, is a title not a surname, and it means anointed one. When using the term Christ Consciousness, we are referencing the Divine Consciousness.)

Nile Valley Temples/Schools
Nile Valley Temples/Schools of Enlightenment were at the center of religion, science, politics, and education, actualizing, excogitating, deriving, and bringing forth the known from the unknown.

According to Anthony Browder, several hundred years before the Greeks successfully conquered Kemet in 332 BC, they studied at the Temples in Kemet learning the Kemetic teachings.

Once Kemet was conquered, Nile Valley Temples / Kemetian Schools of "Mysteries", to outsiders, became known as the Egyptian Mystery Schools/Hermetic Science.

↔

It is imperative to understand history for self-awareness and self-actuality in reaching your greatest potential (using your Spiritual Power from the Knowing). I often state that when the Greeks conquered Kemet, they contributed to the lowering of the vibration of Man, man's existence out of the Divine Consciousness into Human Consciousness, out of alignment with Nature, i.e. the Divine.

↔

When one aligns with the Divine Consciousness in this Dimension of Life, one Lives. When one practices the Universal Laws, one understands the power in aligning with Divinity.

What has been hidden, the 7 Divine Universal Laws, is now revealed. The 7 Divine Universal Laws, which all have borrowed from our Ancestors and knowingly or unknowingly, used or misused.

Your true Greatness is in the use of your power from the Divine Consciousness.

Breathe, You are SPIRIT
Create, You are LIGHT
Transform, You are LOVE

Welcome to *Permission To Be Great*! Enjoy!
~ *Queen Phyllis L-Miata*

Meditation / Quiet Time
Please take this moment to reflect on what you have
just read. Turn within.

Be Enlightened

Part I - Prologue

As given to me by Spirit and the Ancestors, the

LAW OF  LIFE

LAW OF LIFE

**When your
Human Consciousness elevates
into your Divine Consciousness,
When your Ego elevates into your Spirit,
you will have elevated into the Kingdom.**

(When Understanding the Law of Life,
one will increase their Vibration)

**-Queen Miata
NTR God's Messenger**

(Other words used for the Creator: , Laevae, Ngewo, Allah, Jahovah)

Your Greatest Potential

I will operate from Neter, the *Supreme* of me. Let's say this affirmation together 3-times, please.

> I will operate from Neter, the Supreme of me.

> I will operate from Neter, the Supreme of me.

> I will operate from Neter, the Supreme of me.

There is a Supreme of you connecting all of us. Some have referenced it as the Universe, Neter, God, Spirit, Inner voice, and Intuition. However you reference this *Entity*, it represents your *Greatness* and your *Greatest* potential. Here we will connect with this *Entity* using the terms Neter, Spirit, God and Universe.

Today, you start your journey of living and delivering your *Greatest* potential.

Many of you may have heard the term fullest potential, which represents quantity, like a full cup of water. However, the *Greatest* potential represents quality; *is the water fresh, drinkable, nourishing?*

Your fullest potential is all about the quantity of life you choose to operate from and create in your world. However, your *Greatest* potential is about the *quality* of life you choose to operate from and create in your world.

This is your choice.

If you are living a full life, you can choose to live a *great* life. If you are just existing, going to and fro, you can choose to live a *great* life.

The choice is yours, and the power is within you.

The *greatest* of you is infused in the understanding that we are all made in the image and likeness of Netcheru, Divine Universal Principles and Laws. GOD gave each one of us part of his Spirit. And, the Soul is where the Spirit resides in the body.

Notice our referencing of God as male. According to the *Universal Law of Gender*, masculine energy/entities carry and give instructions for a plan, and feminine energy/entities receive, develop, and nurture the instructions given. Hence, God, the Creator – Father, and Mother Earth – nurturer, in neither case are we referencing a person.

However, Neter (NTR) is the Kemetic word for Nature. Neter inherently incorporates all energy, feminine and masculine. Neter references the Divine Force within the Creator's creations (Nature), which is so powerful that it can create, sustain, and maintain Life.

Again, the greatest of you, in other words, your greatness, is infused in the understanding that we are all made in the image and likeness of the Netcheru.

Our human form is a capsule for our Spirit, and our human form allows us to visibly be recognized as a Spirit, a Divine entity.

When I see a human being, I am able to recognize a Spirit. Now, I will say, I don't know if the *Spirit* of the body is at the controls or the *ego*, but, just like a vehicle needs a driver and a house needs tenants for the greatest delivery of its purpose and plan, the *Neter* needs to guide the body for the greatest fulfillment in your life, which is your plan, your purpose.

Imagine this, put a running car in drive and allow it to go without the driver, it will soon stop or crash. Just like a house without tenants, let the power of the house, electricity, water, and gas operate without the control of its occupants, it will soon damage itself.

The house needs a tenant, the car needs a driver, and your body needs the Spirit to ensure the reaching of its *greatest* potential.

With the Ego operator, one will soon reach its degree of the fullest potential and eventually stop, become stagnant, or crash.

Therefore, having a body, which listens to the Neter will ensure that the *greatness* of one's existence is manifested – one's purpose, one's plan, *Divine will*. Just like God (fresh, nourishing water), our Spirit (representing a drop of such water) is equal in quality and resides in our soul. The only difference being the amount (quantity), but given to us by Neter is the *quality of greatness*. We are made in the image and likeness of the Neteru, a Spirit of and connected to *greatness* – Neter, Divinity, existing in you.

Formal and worldly educations can help you reach your fullest potential. However, all the degrees and money in the world will not get you to your greatest potential. And, vice versa, your greatest potential may not utilize your fullest potential. However, your *greatest* potential will definitely be fulfilling and create a state of wholeness.

Here's a real case scenario:
While booking hotel accommodations in NYC, I looked for the best names in the business. However, I believed I could get a better price by utilizing a third party online booking agency than going directly to each hotel site independently.

I put in my specifications: 4 stars, Manhattan and several names were given as the likely possibilities, all of them on my list. How could I go wrong? I knew I was going to get what I wanted. Well, I hit the submit button and got a hotel that was not on the list, of which I never heard. Now, my strategic mind knew, since this wasn't an option presented, I could argue legitimately and reverse the outcome.

My first thought, was seriously. My second thought, from Spirit, knows everything is in Divine Order.

Well, I got to New York, and checked in this unique hotel. I had a craving for some nourishing quality food. I went to the concierge to inquire about a store selling such food and was amazed to find out I was around the corner from a grocery store. Throughout my stay, I realized I was in the perfect location.

When I got on a bus to go uptown to Harlem, I saw my #1 preferred choice of the other hotels, looked at the surroundings, and was more thankful for Divine Intervention. To top it all off, my hotel came in a few hundred dollars less.

YEAH!

Again, your *greatest* potential may not utilize your fullest potential, but it will definitely be fulfilling.

I have come to understand Universal awareness; when you are operating at your fullest potential, you will soon stop or crash.

God cannot use you if you are all tapped out. The Universe cannot use you when you are energy-deprived.

However, when you are operating at your *greatest* potential, the feedback mechanism is one of fulfillment, restoration, and resurrection. Your Divine purpose is creation, Divine creation. The Universe's, Earth's and Life's inherent will, Divine will, is creating, sustaining, and maintaining Life.

↔

Following Spirit is following *your Guide – the Shepherd within.* Learn the voice of the Shepherd within.

23rd Psalm

¹The LORD is my shepherd; I shall not want.

² He maketh me to lie down in green pastures: he leadeth me beside the still waters.

³ He restoreth my soul: he leadeth me in the paths of righteousness for his name's sake.

⁴ Yea, though I walk through the valley of the shadow of death, I will fear no evil: for thou art with me; thy rod and thy staff they comfort me.

⁵ Thou preparest a table before me in the presence of mine enemies: thou anointest my head with oil; my cup runneth over.

⁶ Surely goodness and mercy shall follow me all the days of my life: and I will dwell in the house of the LORD forever.

When one chooses to operate from *Greatness*, Neter's *Spirit* within, *greatness* is their reward.

- ❖ *'The Lord is my Shepherd'* means the Spirit within.
- ❖ *'Shall not want'* means provisions are met.
- ❖ *'Green Pastures'* represents quality – greatness, and *'Still waters'* represents peace.
- ❖ *'He leadeth me in the paths of righteousness for his name's*

sake' represents finding your purpose, fulfilling his purpose, i.e. Divine Will.

❖ *'Yea, though I walk through the valley of the shadow of death, I will fear no evil: for thou art with me; thy rod and thy staff they comfort me'* means you will be protected.

❖ *'My cup runneth over'* represents fulfillment.

❖ *'Surely goodness and mercy shall follow me all the days of my life'* means greatness is delivered to you wherever you go.

When one chooses to operate from *Greatness*, Neter - the Divine Force within, fear is out and power, love, and a sound mind is in. Neter is one of *power*, *love* and a *sound mind.* For God has not given us a Spirit of fear, but of *power* and of *love* and of a *sound mind,* 2 Timothy 1:7.

When you follow Spirit, you will not live in fear, hate, or mental confusion. *When you follow Neter, power, love, knowledge, and wisdom are the rewards.* Studying the 12 Powers of Man (Faith, Love, Strength, Wisdom, Power, Imagination, Understanding, Will, Order, Zeal, Elimination and Life), will give you a better understanding of your Spiritual gifts.

If you feel powerless, which is an inability to create good in your life, if you feel fear, if you feel like you are making bad, stupid decisions, you made the choice to do so; even though, it may have been done unknowingly. It is your choice, and it is self-induced nonsense, s.i.n. It is your choice, your cause, your effect.

In other words, the vehicle is being driven by itself, not the driver. The house is operating by itself, without the tenant. And, the body is moving and thinking for itself by way of the ego; it is not being guided by the Spirit. Therefore, it, the body has or will eventually stop and crash. Fear, hate, anger, weakness, sickness, and jealously are all signs of the body crashing.

What must you do?

You must stop letting the body be the guide of you and start letting the Spirit be the guide of you. Your Spirit and only <u>*your Divine Force within, Neter,*</u> is the best, the *greatest* guide for your plan and your purpose.

Spirit gave me 5 instructions in my role as a Queen:
1) My default must be love.
2) Speak to everyone as if I am speaking to the Spiritual Father.
3) Never argue, debate, or try to convert.
4) Quickly get through my emotions and move forward.
5) Always lookup.

My practice of these 5 Divine Instructions enables my stance in my Divinity. Love, Agape love, is the key to unlocking and elevating the heart, freeing the Spirit from despair, resistance. Thus, allowing one's Spirit to take flight ascending one to the Light, from which one can live. The Divine Force within you is your Light. One must operate from the Divine Force within to Live.

Our Ancestors, tens of thousands of years ago, recognized:

The Heart is the Conscience and Will of Man, the Cause, and the Tongue delivers what is in the Heart; thereby manifesting the Effect. (Heru represents Conscience and Will, Djhuiti represents deliverance and manifestation)
~Understanding The Universal Law of Cause and Effect
(Kemetic Teachings)

The Law of Polarity states that everything exists in duality. According to the *Universal Law of Polarity*, everything is on a continuum and has an opposite. There are two poles or opposites; the difference between the two extremes of one thing is called polarity. For example, cause is in contrast to effect, right is in opposition to left; cold is in polarity to hot.

Existing on Neter's end of the pole is the guiding *Spirit*, health, wholeness, divine order, and the 12 powers/gifts of man.

On the opposite end of the pole, is the guiding body, the Ego, fear, hate, mental confusion, things opposite the 12 powers of man.

Freewill means you have a choice in your existence.

Which pole will you gravitate towards and choose to BE?

From which pole will you operate?

When you choose *Spirit* as your *Guide*, surely goodness and mercy shall follow you all the days of your life, and you are divinely powered up to create greatness in your life. There is no void.

If a void exists in your world, in your mental, physical and emotional beings, know there is no void in Neter. Understand your Divinity. Go into your Divinity. Turn within and utilize the *greatest* of you, the *greatness* in you – *Spirit.* Turn within and access your gifts. They were given to you upon your conception.

If they remain unopened, why?

If they remain unused, why?

For Neter is of power, love and a sound mind.

Real case example
As I have professed recently, I live in a world of being nice, being loving and cherished friendship. I will not join others exist-

ing in and on the opposite poles of Spiritual guidance. Seriously, why would I? I don't prescribe to S.I.N. (Self – Induced nonsense - SIN).

↔

The story of Job is a story of…*what if Neter did not give us the Spirit of power, love and a sound mind…*such is the story of Job.

If Neter did not give us its *Spirit of Power*, we, like Job, would face perils, sickness, and death, which are represented in life by a state of stagnation, the inability to grow and flourished, and the inability to create good in your life.   The enemy, the Ego, or any adversary on the opposite pole of God would reign over your life, including sickness, poverty, dis-ease, and disease.   You open yourself up to this madness when the body is driving itself.   You will not have a polar end of God to go to if Neter did not give us its *Spirit*, which is being made in the image and likeness of Neteru.

According to Physics, we know two things cannot occupy the same space at the same time. Sickness and Neter cannot exist at the same time. It is not Neter's desire for you to be sick.   Your belief in Neter at the same time giving power to any adversary of Neter is not a Divine principle.

Once Job realized he was made in the image and likeness of Neter, Job turned to the Spirit of Neter and professed the truth-Neter is omnipotent and Job was renewed.

As with Job, you must remember you are made in the image and likeness of Neter. The opposite of Neter, the enemy and sickness cannot exist where Neter is...*for Neter's Spirit is of power, love and a sound mind.*

Real Case scenario
I do not profess sick days. When I take off, I am taking a healing

day - a day of rest, relaxation, renewing and restoration. At any given time, I listen to Neter to tell me what my body needs. I choose to submit to the Guidance of Neter, its Spirit within. I praise Neter for giving me its Spirit. I understand this; Neter and its adversaries (sickness, poverty, mental illness…) are not roommates.   There is no threesome in my body only Neter and I, which I refer to as SI (the Spirit in I).

↔

Lastly, **Peter** was fearful of walking on the water. Peter in his Human consciousness could not see the possibility of doing what Spirit, represented by Jesus the Christ, wanted him to do. Such is **the story of Peter**…the story of Human consciousness not being Spiritual Divine Consciousness.

In Human consciousness, as Peter was, you will experience fear and anxiety. When you turn towards, listen, and stay focus on Spirit, Christ consciousness, you will be able to overcome your fear and anxiety and do those things Spirit calls you to do.

Get your Human consciousness out of the way. Spirit is calling you to do the things equating to walking on water, things you thought you could not do when Spirit told you to do them.

When Peter flipped flopped back to his Human consciousness, fear and anxiety prevailed. However, when he turned backed to his Spiritual consciousness as taught by Christ, he had expanded his Spiritual understanding and elevated his Spiritual power as represented by his ability to heal.

<u>The Law of Life</u>

*When your Human Consciousness elevates into
your Divine Consciousness, When your Ego elevates into
your Spirit, You will have elevated into the Kingdom.*

(When understanding the Law of Life, one will increase their vibration)

~ Queen Miata

As with Peter, overcome your fear by listening to the Spirit of Neter within you to Guide you. You can do exceedingly marvelous things. Practice meditation, being quiet, and learn the voice of the Spirit, the Shepherd. Listen to the Shepherd, the Christ within...you shall not want. I use a very powerful practice of Neter developed through the Spirit in I (SI) called *Alignment of Consciousness.*

↔

Eating well facilitates one's ability to hear and listen to the Spirit within. Eat well. Better yet, eat life, organic high frequency foods. One thing learned from others and experienced, there is a correlation between proper nourishment and Spiritual enlightenment and elevation. It is easier to be more emotional when you have chemicals and toxins in your body – when the body is not balanced or relaxed. When you balance your body with proper nourishment, lessening the toxins and chemicals within, it will be easier to become quiet, less emotional, meditate, align with the Divine Consciousness, and stay in high vibration.

Additionally, Sunlight nourishes the body providing energy and other health benefits keeping the body in high vibration. Blacks need 2-4 hours of Sunlight due to selenium-based melanin and other nutritional benefits of Sunlight.
(Do your research on the nutritional needs of Blacks, alkaline foods, Sunlight, Selenium-based melanin, etc. It is common practice, especially in America, to based nutritional needs on Caucasian norms.

Continuing, the Spirit of Neter will not only tell you what to eat, the Spirit of Neter will dress you and tell you what to wear, what to say, and will teach you a lesson on being quiet. You will learn how to properly create your world of Greatness with your praise, which are your words and your actions. The junk from your body of emotions and your ego will decrease in your thoughts, your words, and your actions. What will increase are good words, uplifting words, praise in your words and actions.

Question:
How do you know you are hearing from Neter?

Here's the answer… Remember, Neter will not be in conflict with itself. If you are sensing anything opposite of Neter's pole: such as fear, weakness, or powerlessness, then this is not *of Neter*. Therefore, this is not *with Neter*.

According to research, the Spirituality center is located in the right hemisphere of the brain. Because the right hemisphere of the brain controls the left side of the body, it is the belief that Spirit speaks to one in the left ear.

Real case scenario
Being one who hears from and listens to Spirit, I was amazed that the voice of Spirit does come through on my left side - my left ear.

Your *greatest* life is at hand, because it is in your hands. It is your choice. Neter never left you. Turn within; your state of Heaven (greatness) or hell (only fullness) on this Earth is a choice.

Real case vision
I call Earth the playground for the Spirits. The image I have is looking out of the 2nd-floor window of our Chicago flat. Looking down at the kids playing on and in the streets, asking my mother, may I go play? However, before I go, she gives me the dos and don'ts, reminding me I am Spirit. I may be in the world, but I am not of the world.

Being a child with a child's level of understanding and discernment, when I returned, my mother cleansed the sweet play of Human consciousness from my mind. Any fear and negative thoughts, which may have attached, are gone before I go to bed, and I awake reborn in my Spiritual consciousness.

My Spiritual enlightenment has led me to choose and submit to and follow Neter - my Guide – my Shepherd. As a parent, I taught my children that they are *of God,* this being their truth, their first and true identity.

I choose to operate from *Greatness*, the Spirit of Neter within me. I choose my *greatest* potential.

↔

The Netcher, God, and the Universe are calling you to choose your *Greatest* potential. Operate from *Supreme greatness*, the Neter within you.

> I will operate from Neter, the Supreme of me.

> I will operate from Neter, the Supreme of me.

> I will operate from Neter, the Supreme of me.

This is '*Permission to be Great'*, your world being your connection to Netcheru through Spirit, through the Neter within you.

With *Love, Life* and *Light* be the expression of Neter's Goodness, and light up your world by operating from the *Greatest* of you, the *Greatness* in you, the NETER of you.

Next up, the Seven Essential Spiritual Principles of Self,
HOUSEHOLD DNA

Breathe, I AM SPIRIT
Create, I AM LIGHT
Transform, I AM LOVE

Meditation / Quiet Time
Please take this moment to reflect on what you have
just read. Turn within.

RISE!

Part II - The Seven Essential Spiritual Principles of Self, i.e. Household DNA

WEHEME MESU - REBIRTHS
The Kemetic term Weheme Mesu means
Repetition of the Births.

THE 7 SPIRITUAL PRINCIPLES of SELF
& THE HOUSEHOLD DNA MIR
The Divine Consciousness, i.e. The 5th Dimension

The Divine Consciousness is a Consciousness of Life, and it starts with the Spiritual Principle of Love (~528 Hz).

All Healing and Ascension begin in the Heart. The practice of Agape Love elevates the vibration of the Heart. Agape Love is the key to unlocking the Heart, freeing the Spirit from any despair, trauma, and unforgiveness.

The Spirit takes flight ascending one to the Light, the Divine Force within, from which one Lives.

Agape Love gives rise to elevated States of Beings in which one exists.

1 Essential Spiritual Principle of Self

Love

There is a Supreme of you connecting all of us. Some have referenced it as the Universe, Neter, God, Spirit, Inner voice, and Intuition. However you reference this *Entity*, it represents your Greatness and your *greatest* potential. Here we will connect with this *Entity* using the terms Neter, Spirit, God and Universe.

DNA represents the fundamentals behind outward noticeable expressions. Genetic DNA reference information carried on genes, which are expressed in living organisms. A higher understanding of DNA is that DNA carries the memories of past generations. This is why outward expressions can skip generations; it is also why emotions (comfort and trauma) can pass from one generation to another. Just like Genetic DNA, the term Household DNA, in this usage, represents the fundamentals of what can and is being expressed in and throughout our Households.

There are 7 Essential Spiritual Principles of Self embodied in Household DNA. The Mir edifice, a symbol of Spiritual connectedness, was divinely given to me as the structural form to use to display these principles, for the most obvious reason I believe. The structural strength of the Mir has stood the test of time, and these seven spiritual principles will stand the test of time in our households. In addition, the apex of the MiR represents ASCENSION

The color associated with each principle represents one of the *12 Powers of Man*. This associated power is needed to deliver a greater understanding of the Household DNA corresponding principle.

These 7 Essential Spiritual Principles of Self are the fundamentals to expressing greatness in and throughout your household.

↔

*The First Principle of Household DNA is **Agape Love**.*

Neter is Love and so am I.

Neter is Love and so am I.

Neter is Love and so am I.

Love is a gift given to us by Neter and is one of the 12 powers of man. Love gives us the ability to attract, unify and *transform*.

Neter's love is a devoted and committed love. When you choose to love regardless of feelings, motivations, or emotions, you are practicing Agape love – Neter's love.

Agape love is the key to unlocking and elevating the heart, freeing the Spirit from despair, trauma, unforgiveness, and other resistance. The Spirit takes flight ascending one to the Light, from which one can live. The Divine Force within you is your Light. One must operate from the Divine Force within to Live.

Agape love represents three functions of Household DNA. Pictured in the Mir:

1) Agape love is the base - the foundation of the Household DNA Mir on which the other six principles stand. The foundation of an entity determines its inherent power and strength. Neter is love, and *love is transformative power.*

2) Agape love is a support beam of the Mir. Operating from Neter brings you into the *Love State of Being*; you become '*of Love*'.

3) Agape love is daily nourishment represented on the sides of the Mir structure. Exhibiting a daily behavior of Agape love feeds and strengthens our soul and the souls of others.

The color associated with Love on the Household DNA Mir is red, which represents the *Power of Life*. Here, the *Spiritual Power of Life* is circulated when we operate in Love, Neter's Love – Agape Love.

God is Love (1 John 4:8) and so am I (1 John 4:7).

Neter being omnipotent, the most powerful force in the Universe, means Love is the most powerful force in the Universe.

When you know that you are unconditionally love, your life comes alive. You are energized, invigorated and rejuvenated. You are even more loving.

Thoughts create, but *love transforms*. Love transforms a person - energizing them, giving them life.

Love someone and see them become energized, see them come to life. See them transformed.

An activated power of man when one comes to life, when one comes alive, when one becomes energized, is the *Power of Zeal*. Zeal is the ability to be passionate, motivated and enthusiastic.

Talk about transformation and resurrection.

Love someone unconditionally and see life exalt, see zeal manifest, see one become invigorated and energized, see one become more enthusiastic and passionate…

Neter is Love and so am I.

A new commandment I give to you (John 13:34), *that you love one another; as I have loved you, that you also love one another.*

Love is defined as a deep affection, devotion.

There are 5 types of Loves:

1) Epithumia Love – Physical Desire
2) Eros Love – Romance
3) Storge Love – Natural Affection
4) Phileo Love – Cherished Friendship
5) Agape Love – Unconditional Love

Epithumia, eros, storge, and phileo loves require the sense or feeling of affection, passion. Epithumia, eros, storge, and phileo loves are loves of emotions, emotionally they come and emotionally they go. If at times you believe you do not love your family or your household members, it is because you are loving them from your emotions, from the ego, the body side of you.

However, Agape love is unconditional. It is Agape love that operates by choosing to love, choosing to be loving towards others. And, Agape love is the only love inherently sustainable and maintainable because it is connected to Spirit, which is always with you.

Many people will seek love and seek to love based on their feelings. However, there are fewer people who know the true power of Agape love, loving another individual unreservedly and without expectations. Agape love requires a greater Spiritual understanding because Agape love represents the love

Neter has for us. Agape love is a choice, not a feeling because one has a choice in following Neter. Regardless of one's choosing, Neter works the same in all, choosing to love us unconditionally.

You can choose to love all the time regardless of motivations or other emotions. When you practice this kind of love, you are demonstrating Agape love. Agape love is the type of love that must be practiced in the household. Bring and enhance life in your household by practicing Agape love.

Agape love is strengthening, powerful, curative, encouraging, uplifting and transformative. When household members practice Agape love towards one another, household members will be strengthened, empowered, healed, encouraged, uplifted and transformed. Agape love breathes Life.

Neter is light, and light is love. If you are moving in Neter, exhibiting Neter, you are exhibiting Agape love. Agape love is the light you must operate from to create a *strong loving family*. Agape love unifies individuals to become one.

This is the *Power of Agape love*, exalting life unconditionally without expectations.

Agape love is shown by what it is: devotion, goodwill, benevolence and kindness. Agape love is not based on how one looks, what one does or did, where one was born, who birth one or how one feels. True unconditional love is Neter - Agape love. And, Neter does not base its love for us, which is given to us, on how we look, where we were born, who birth us, or what we did or do.

Regardless of any and all circumstances, irrespective of who you are, what you do or have done, Neter's love for you is everlasting. Neter's love resides in us. Neter's love speaks to us through Spiritual guidance, and it is always there for us to tap into and use.

The love of Neter, Neter's love for you, and the love you are is to be expressed out of your soul from your Spirit; it is to radiate through your body, and it is to be delivered as praise through your words and actions, resurrecting and restoring your loved ones, manifesting in the Universe, unifying, and connecting all as '*One*'.

Neter is love and so are you. You are made in the image and likeness of Neter's love for us. The love of Neter exists in you.

You are love and you are loved.

You are love and you are loved.

You are love and you are loved.

Agape love was given to you in your Spirit. Agape love is created from the Spirit within.

According to the *Universal Law of Polarity*, everything is on a continuum and has an opposite. There are two poles or opposites; the difference between the two extremes of one thing is called polarity.

On the polar end of Neter, consist of knowing Neter is consistent, everlasting, omniscient, omnipresent and omnipotent. Neter being love means Neter's love, Agape love, is consistent, everlasting, always present, and very powerful.

On the opposite polar end of Neter, consist of fear, anxiety, and the emotional loves: phileo, epithumia, storge and eros. Inherently, they are inconsistent and unstable.

Therefore, Agape love is the only love that is inherently sustainable and maintainable because it is connected to Spirit, which is always with you.

Move in NETER.
*Operate on Neter's polar end.
Listen to Spiritual guidance.

Understanding of the principle of the Law of Polarity enables one to change his own Polarity, as well as that of others.

> *In essence, <u>one has the power to transform oneself and others from one pole to the other</u> if one devotes the time and study necessary to master the art by concentrating upon the opposite pole to that which you desire to suppress.*
> *–The Kybalion*

In this matter, one is to concentrate on Agape Love.

You may ask, how is this done?

Well, it starts with your thoughts. Thoughts have power, energy associated with them.

In my Physics' class, I demonstrate to students this energy by elevating a pendulum in my hand and having it move, cycling to the left and then to the right. This is due to the thoughts in my mind generating nerve impulses in my brain, which transport energy radiating through my arm, fingers and the pendulum. The cycling of energy is due to the gravitational pull on Earth causing rotation.

The *Universal law of Mentalism* is based on the power of thoughts. What you think has energy, which cycles and affects others around you, as well as you. In addition, we move through our thoughts. Your words and actions are expressions of your thoughts.

As I often tell my grandchild, change your thoughts, change your mindset; change your mindset, change your circumstance.

You can choose with whom and with what your thoughts align. Aligning with Neter's side of the pole is power, love and a sound mind. Keep your mind stayed on Neter. Listen to Spiritual guidance. Neter has not given us nor is it the Spirit of fear.

Knowing this means when you operate from Neter's polar end, listening to Spiritual guidance, and from Neter's love, you become a strong powerful transformative agent enhancing the life of others.

Remember, if thoughts create and love transforms, then loving thoughts are the most powerful transformative agents.

Recall:
1) Agape Love is the foundation. Inherently you have transformative power.

2) Agape Love is a *State of Being*. Be alive, be energized. Every day, every hour, every minute, and every second Neter/God is loving you. Live your life as Love knowing that you are loved.

3) Agape Love is daily nourishment exhibited in your daily behavior. Your words and your actions are feedback mechanisms to resurrect and elevate the self, you. They are also transformative agents to resurrect and elevate others.

Illuminate Neter's light by illuminating Neter's love.

Recognize the Spirit of Neter residing in others through your expression of Agape love towards them.

Resurrect your soul, and elevate your household by radiating Neter's love in your praise; yours words and your actions are your praise.

The Universe is calling you to be the transformative power you are.   As we are all part of the *Universal Consciousness of One*, Love unifies us. Love gives life.

The accompanied associate to *Agape Love* is *Giving*. Through Agape loving behavior, your ability to give increases.

↔

Neter is Love and so am I.

Neter is Love and so am I.

Neter is Love and so am I!

Next up: Household DNA's 2nd Principle -
PEACE

Breathe, I AM SPIRIT
Create, I AM LIGHT
Transform, I AM LOVE

Meditation / Quiet Time
Please take this moment to reflect on what you have
just read. Turn within.

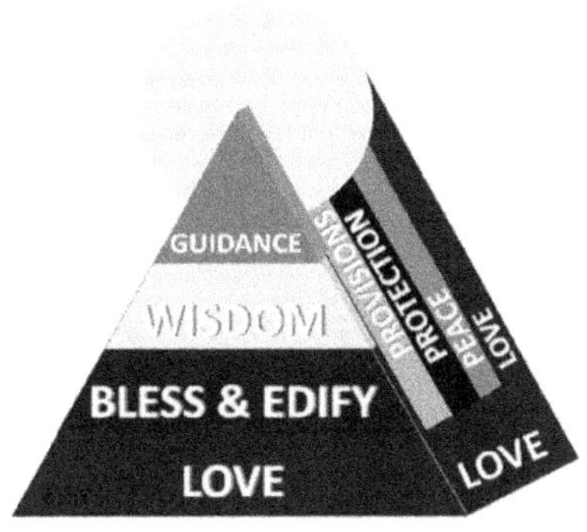

2nd Essential Spiritual Principle of Self

Peace

The support beams on the corners of the Household DNA Mir represent the *Principles of the States of Beings.* These principles: *Love, Peace, Protection,* and *Provisions* radiate out of the foundation of Neter/God's love, the transformative power giving rise to these *States of Beings.*

↔

*The Second Principle of Household DNA is **Peace.***

Neter is of Peace; I am Neter's agent of Peace.

Neter is of Peace; I am Neter's agent of Peace.

Neter is of Peace; I am Neter's agent of Peace.

According to Isaiah 26:3, *thou wilt keep him in perfect peace, whose mind is stayed on thee: because he trusteth in thee.*

Peace functions as a support beam of the Household DNA Mir. Operating from Neter, the Divine Force within, brings you into the *Peace* state of being.

The color associated with Peace on the Household DNA Mir is gold, which represents the *Power of Understanding.* Here, one must go into *Spiritual Understanding* to get into the state of being of peace and operate in the state of being of peace.

What is peace?

Peace is *Quiet Goodness.*

When we discuss peace in the household, we have to examine two areas where peace needs to exist:

1) one being within self
2) the other being within the household

Let's examine the peace within one's self – within you.

Remember the *Universal Law of Polarity*?

On Neter's pole, there's peace, actually perfect peace coming through the Soul from the Spirit. On the opposite end, other than Neter, there's conflict.

When you align yourself with Neter, you will have perfect peace. Perfect peace is a condition of freedom from disturbance within the soul. It is perfect harmony reigning within.

Getting to peace requires the understanding of one's highest good. Therefore, one can reach a state of perfect peace when you allow *Neter* to guide you, thereby, trusting in thee.

What does this mean?

Simply put, it means that to get to peace, get to your '*Highest Good*'. Ask yourself, when in a so call state of conflict, what is my highest good? Then, turn within, listen to Spirit. Inherently, peace will come from knowing what to do to resolve the conflict in your highest good.

Peace is quiet goodness, knowing unequivocally and without doubt that Spirit operates in your best interest at your highest good.

Conflict really is a state of not knowing what your highest good is. When one engages in conflict, one is positioning for an understanding outside of one's self. Once you comprehend that the Divine Understanding of one's highest good is to be sought from within, real resolution has been initiated. And, once *Spirit* enlightens you on your highest good, giving instructions as to what to do and how, resolution is revealed. Now, peace is a choice you have to make.

Do you continue to engage in the conflict, s.i.n. (self-induced nonsense - sin), or do you enter the *State of Being of Peace* by listening to *Spirit*?

Peace is a choice, and it is attainable.

Right now, at this very moment, if you are in conflict, you can stop and choose to listen to Neter, getting to a *State of Perfect Peace*. You may need to remove yourself from the outside triggers contributing to the conflict. However, please note that if you are in conflict, you too are a trigger.

When you listen to Neter, this is referred to as achieving *Peace with Neter* by refocusing on Neter and listening. Reaching a state of peace with Neter demonstrates the quality of Neter – perfection, perfect peace.

If you continue to keep your mind stayed on Thee (Neter) allowing Spiritual Guidance, you will reach a consistent condition – a *state of perfect peace*. This act of achieving the *Peace of Neter* by the continued practice of focusing on Neter and listening elicits a perpetual state of the *Peace of Neter*, which passeth all understanding (Philippians 4:7). This Peace *of Neter* validates the quantity of Neter's perfect peace - the *State of Being in Peace*.

God is a God of peace (Philippians 4:9). Therefore, when you allow Neter's spirit within you to guide you, you become an agent of peace, a Neter's agent of peace.

According to the Kybalion, understanding of the principle of the *Law of Polarity* enables one to change his own polarity, as well as that of others, if he will devote the time and study necessary to master the art by concentrating upon the opposite pole to that which you desire to suppress.

In this matter, one is to concentrate on peace not conflict.

As Neter's agent of peace demonstrating the most powerful force in the world - love, you have transformative power to transform a house of conflict to peace and facilitate the maintaining of a peaceful household. Peace and conflict exist as polar opposites. Neter's polar end includes peace. Conflict is at the other end, the non-Neter polar end. As a transformative power, one can change the polarity of others from conflict to peace. However, to do this effectively, one must be in peace grounded in Spiritual love – Agape love.

Remember, you are the transformative power for peace in your household.

You carried the power of love to maintain a household of peace and move a household from conflict to peace because you are '*of Neter*'. Neter is love, and the Neter of peace resides in you.

Now that you know this, use your transformative power. Engage in peaceful loving actions to diffuse conflict in the home. Any grievance is conflict. Any conflict (small or large) needs to be resolved and you as the transformative agent want to change the polarity from one of conflict to one of peace. You do this by having the highest good in mind as the result for the persons involved.

Again, you do this by having the highest good in mind as the result for the persons involved in the conflict.

Here's the best starting point for the greatest good…it is a question…ask each party involved, *what will be the highest good for you in resolving this matter that would be aligned with your Divine Spirit?*

Notice how the question allows the person involved to position their mind on Spirit. Listen to the question again. *What will be the highest good for you in resolving this matter that would be aligned with your Divine Spirit?*

The environment may be in separate rooms or the parties may be in the same room, writing their answers or speaking. However, notice that the answer is really independent of the other person's involvement. The answer for each person is going to be based on their Divine Spirit, which in reality is the same Spirit, the Spirit of Neter.

Therefore, we already know the answer, if each person is honest, is going to be in peace because Neter cannot be in conflict with itself. Neter is the same in both parties. The answer from the Neter of one party will not be in conflict with the answer from the Neter from the other party. Now the answers may be different, but the answers will not exist on the same pole to be opposite or in conflict, grievance, with one another.

For example
Suppose father and son are in grievance about using the car. Father's answer is to be home by 8 pm while son desires to be

home by 11 pm. The continuum of time exists on the same pole therefore causing the conflict. If this was the case, Spirit would be in conflict with itself. Therefore, someone or both are not operating in spiritual guidance. Remember, Neter is <u>of Peace</u>. Neter will not be in conflict with itself.

Continuing, after each consults with Spirit, the father's spiritual answer could be to have an older sibling accompany the son on the outing, and the son's spiritual answer could be, to be home by 9 pm. Both being doable and not in conflict.

Gandhi and Dr. King both used this practice. Against violence and hate, they practiced peace and love respectively – both representing Neter's polar end.

When you meet conflict with conflict, you stay at the polar end opposite of peace, opposite of Neter.

Mother Teresa stated, *"I will never attend an anti-war rally; if you have a peace rally, invite me."*

Hence, the real resolution to achieving peace is the *quality* of the peace derived *with Neter*. You want to move the parties to the *Supreme Being's* polar end, where peace exists - the polar end of Neter.

Mother Teresa also stated, *"If we have no peace, it is because we have forgotten that we belong to each other."*

Remember, the spirit inside of each one of us is the Spirit connecting all of us. We are all *One*. We are all a part of the *Universal Consciousness of One*. Energy cycles; therefore, what we do to one individually, we do to all collectively.

The ongoing consistent practice of resolution with the *Peace of Neter* inherently increases and expands the quantity of *Peace* in the home, which facilitates the *State of Peace* being in the home.

The Universe is calling you to be an agent of peace.

The accompanied companion to *Peace* is *Prosperity*. Peace brings greater prosperity. Prosperity elevates in an environment of Peace.

↔

Neter is of Peace; I am Neter's agent of Peace.

Neter is of Peace; I am Neter's agent of Peace.

Neter is of Peace; I am Neter's agent of Peace.

Next up: Household DNA's 3rd Principle -
PROTECTION

Breathe, I AM SPIRIT
Create, I AM LIGHT
Transform, I AM LOVE

Meditation / Quiet Time
Please take this moment to reflect on what you have
just read. Turn within.

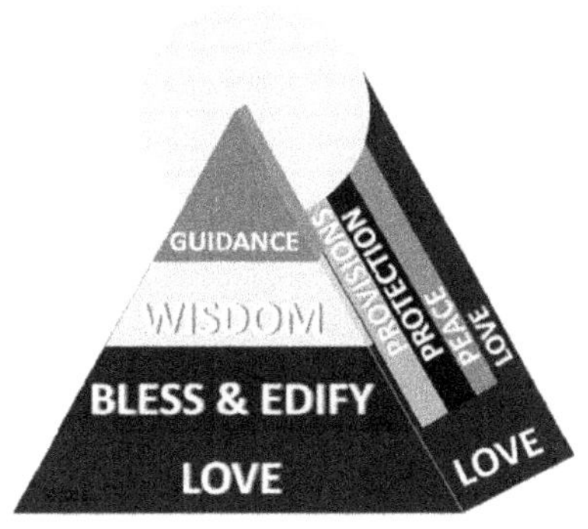

3ʳᵈ Essential Spiritual Principle of Self

Protection

The Third Principle of Household DNA is **Protection**.

Neter's word is pure. I will trust in it; it is my shield.

Neter's word is pure. I will trust in it; it is my shield.

Neter's word is pure. I will trust in it; it is my shield.

Every word of God is pure, Proverbs 30:5; *he is a shield unto them that put their trust in him.*

Protection - safeguard, shield... Protection - to strengthen and preserve the mental, physical, and emotional well-beings, which enhance the hearing of Neter's Spirit in the guidance and purpose in one's life...

Protection functions as a support beam of the Household DNA Mir. Operating from Neter brings you into the *State of Being of Protection.*

The color associated with *Protection* on the Household DNA Mir is dark blue, which represents the *Power of Faith.* Here, one must go into the *Spiritual* understanding of *Faith* to get to the *State of Being of Protection* and to operate in the *State of Being of Protection.*

Your greatest protection is not associated with guns, locks, bars, or alarm systems. Your greatest protection is in your alignment with Neter to strengthen and preserve your mental, physical, and emotional wellness. This enhances your ability to hear and listen to Neter's spirit in the guidance and purpose in your life.

This is the *Faith* that you must have, the belief in the unseen.

Simply stated in 1 Corinthians 2:5, *that your Faith should not stand in the wisdom of men, but in the power of God.*

Faith does not come all at once. It grows.

The journey to protection begins with the knowing that Neter is love. Therefore, Neter's words are pure love, Agape love, and love is the greatest transformative power.

The key to protection is being observant to what is going on in your environment and the power bringing thoughts into visible manifestation.

Let's repeat this because this is very important.

The key to protection is, in essence, discerning what is being created around you. Please apprehend this truth, the environment is always evolving. And, it will be up to your mental, physical, and emotional awareness to tap into these changes.

Therefore, we start with an understanding of energy because energy creates.

God is light (1 John 1:5), and light is energy. Therefore, *God is Energy*. According to the Pert Em Heru and Medu Neter inscriptions, over 5000+ years old, Neter is Energy; Neter is Light.

The most popular equation in the world is $E = mc^2$. 'E' represents pure Energy; mc^2 represents the equivalent of energy when associated with matter, *you*. Matter would have to move at the speed of light squared to be converted into pure energy.

$E = mc^2$ is associated with the *Universal law of Vibration*.

> *"Nothing rests; everything moves; everything vibrates."*
> *-- Djhuiti, Kemetic Teachings*

According to the *Universal Law of Vibration*, everything is vibrating at one speed or another. When we go down on a sub-atomic level, we do not find matter but pure energy. Everything is energy. You are energy, and you vibrate; remember this.

The amount of energy associated with your mass is very very very huge! You are huge amounts of energy compacted in your small amount of body mass.

In essence, you are very powerful.

How powerful is a little bit of Netcheru's pure energy within you?

Here's an example from Pbs.org nova
If you could turn every one of the atoms in a paper clip, which has a mass of less than 1 gram, into pure energy—leaving no mass whatsoever—the paper clip would yield 18 kilotons of TNT. That's roughly the size of the bomb that destroyed Hiroshima in 1945. On Earth, however, there is no practical way to convert a paper clip or any other object entirely to energy. It

would require temperatures and pressures greater than those at the core of our sun.

At 140 lbs., my mass is 64 kg; that is 64,000 grams. And, the pure energy associated with me, based on $E=mc^2$, is over 1.3 million ktons of energy.

With Neter being omnipotent, this is not hard to realize. As we are made in the image and likeness of Netcheru, with a little bit of Netcheru's energy in us, we are truly powerful; you are truly powerful. However, we must protect, enhance, and maintain our ability to be powerful, which is allowing Neter's will in us to work through us for us and not use our energy for self-destruction or the destruction of others.

Again, we must not use our energy for self-destruction.

↔

Energy is the ability to do work.
(Three basic concepts of Energy: Energy vibrates at a certain frequency; Energy aligns with Energy based on similar frequencies; Energy is neither created nor destroyed, it transforms from one type to another.)

Work = Force x displacement.

Power is work/time.

Neter means the Divine Force within. Referencing the above equations, Force is needed for Power. A force is a push or pull, a push or pull in and on the Universe creates.

Simply put, your power depends on the amount of work you do in a certain amount of time. You have the energy and the power to do work, which is to create your world.

Hear this - we think about 1 thought per 1.2 seconds, over 70,000 thoughts per day. Some thoughts we cancel out, and others we keep. Thoughts have energy associated with them vibrating at a certain frequency. We move through our thoughts, creating our world with our words and actions. Words and actions have energy associated with them at certain frequencies.

There are only two types of worlds you can create: 1) a life-enhancing world on the polar end of Neter, or 2) a life-hindering world on the opposite polar end of Neter.

A life hindering world leads to death and destruction. In essence, death and destructive thoughts do not transform into life exalting words and actions. It is nonsensical to curse your child or household members thinking you are enriching the positive creative power within them and in your household magnifying life. Death and destructive words and actions do not transform into life.

Neter is love, and Neter's love doesn't curse. Neter's love of transforming power builds life. Neter's words are pure in love and energy, unfiltered.   All that energy is all that power in you for you to use. Neter gives us the Spirit of power, love, and a sound mind.

↔

The highest level of Human vibration occurs when you get you out of the way and allow Neter to guide and work through you.

Let's repeat.

The highest level of human vibration occurs when you get out of your way and allow Neter to guide you and work through you. And, the opposite is true. The lowest level of human vibration occurs in people at the opposite polar end of Neter - those individuals not being guided by Neter, but who are guided by self, the *ego*.

You do not want to be around very low vibrating people for obvious reasons. Yes, you treat them with Agape love recognizing their Divine spirit. However, having these individuals in your inner circle of companions is life-threatening.

For example
That friend who curses everyone out or gets angry very quickly... Is he or she listening to Neter and allowing Neter to work in him or her? NO! And, this person is operating at a low frequency... not at Neter's end of the pole but at the other end opposite Neter's pole, where chaos, confusion, life-hindering attributes reside – where life-impeding less protective attributes reside.

↔

What stops one from hearing and receiving Neter's *words and acting with the power one is given and has?*

It is the compromising of one's mental, physical, and/or emotional states.

For example
-Get stressed out with debt, one will be emotionally unstable (not at peace) to hear Neter.
-Eat a lot sugar and develop diabetes, one will be in a physical state of dis-ease (not at peace) to hear Neter.
-Under the influence, one will be not of a sound mind (not of a mental state) to hear Neter.

Negative mental, physical, and emotional states are obstructions in hearing the word of Neter. And, when you can't hear the word of Neter, you can't listen to the word of Neter. It is only a matter of time before you engage in self-destructive behavior – S.I.N (Self-Induced Nonsense).

The God of my rock; in him will I trust (2 Samuel 22:3); he is my shield, and the horn of my salvation, my high tower, and my refuge, my saviour; thou savest me from violence.

Again, it is very difficult to trust a God you cannot hear.

When household members are positioned or moving away from Neter's polar end, their mental, physical, and emotional well-beings are compromised. They are not hearing or listening to Spirit. And, as they move farther away from Neter's polar end, they move further into self, self-induced nonsense. Self-induced nonsense inherently decreases protection. It is difficult to stay in Divinity when you cannot hear what Neter is telling you to do.

Internally, your household must strengthen and enhance the mental, physical, and emotional well-beings of the family household members. Protecting the body and household means to monitor what comes in and what is allow to reside in the body and in the household.

For example
Neter doesn't curse. Cursing impedes/stops the hearing of Neter. Neter's words are pure love.

Speak agape-loving words.
Do agape-loving actions.
Think agape-loving thoughts.

Remember, words and actions are expressions of our thoughts. We move through our thoughts.

If you find it difficult to control your thoughts, then check your heart. The Heart is one's Conscience and Will, the Cause, from which thoughts, words, and actions are created. To open and elevate the heart into a higher vibration one must use Agape love. Agape love is the key to unlocking and elevating the heart, freeing the Spirit from despair, trauma, unforgiveness (low vibrations). The Spirit takes flight ascending one to the Light from which one can live.

Therefore, move into Agape love to help you move towards Neter, your light, aligning with your light. This will enhance the hearing of Spirit, Neter speaking to you. When you can hear what Neter is telling you, you can do what Neter is telling you to do. When you can hear what Neter is telling you, you can trust Neter to guide you and be your Shepherd.

Every word of Neter is pure; it is a shield unto them that put their trust in it.

↔

Additionally, you must eat for life; eat organic high frequency foods. Processed foods and bad eating habits are obstacles to hearing the word of Neter. Again, eat for life by eating high frequency organic foods.

Protection is increased from the inside out, starting with your heart, to your thoughts, to your words, to your actions. You want your family hearts, your family thoughts, your family words, and your family actions to be *Divine, of Neter.*

According to the *Principle of Attraction,* which is part of the broader understanding of the *Universal Laws of Vibration and Mentalism*, what you think, what you speak, and what you do is what you will attract, what will manifest in your world. This is because Energy aligns with Energy based on similar frequencies.

-Good in, good out; good out, good in
-Love in, love out; love out, love in
-Conflict in, conflict out; conflict out, conflict in
-Violence in, violence out; violence out, violence in

Therefore, every family member in their goings, comings and interactions, will enhance the mental, physical, and emotional well-beings of the household and its members or will hinder the mental, physical, and emotional well-beings of the household and its members.

This needs to be repeated.

Every family member, in their goings, comings and interactions, will either enhance or hinder the mental, physical, and emotional well-beings of the household and its members.

Children do not have the level of discernment as that of an adult. For that reason, children will mimic what they see.

According to the *Universal Law of Cause and Effect*, there are consequences for our actions, otherwise known as KARMA (Kemetic principle).

> *"Every Cause has its Effect; every Effect has its Cause; everything happens according to Law; There is no Chance, Chance is but a name for Law not recognized; there are many planes of causation, but nothing escapes the Law."*   -- *Djhuiti, Kemetic Teachings*

(Note: Newton's first and third laws of motion are derived from the Kemetic Laws of Vibration and Cause and Effect respectively. Newton's second law of motion is based on the Kemetic concepts of force.)

In basic terms, the Universal Law of Cause and Effect indicates that *for every action there is a reaction*…or in Layman's term: What goes around, comes around; what you put out, you will surely get back.

Real case scenario
When I was a teenaged driver, I hit a car and left. About 2-3yrs. later, someone struck my car and left the scene. My first thought was, 'Balance in the Universe'.

The Universe will balance itself out. Overall, what the household puts out, the household gets back.

As we increase our vibration, mentally rising in our thoughts, we understand our power as *Causers*.

We are all connected in the *Cycle of Life*. And, every family member, in their goings, comings, actions, and interactions is responsible for the well-being, the PROTECTION, of the household members. Thus, any type of tradition, action, word, or habit that erodes and destroys the mental, physical, and emotional wellness of the household members must not enter or be allowed to reside in the household or body of the household members. They must be eradicated with Neter's pure energy of Agape love in our thoughts, words and actions.

According to the *Universal Law of Polarity*, everything is on a continuum and has an opposite. There are two poles or opposites. The difference between the two extremes of one thing is called polarity: non-violence is opposite to violence; peace and war are opposites.

Understanding of the *Principle of the Law of Polarity* enables one to change his own polarity, as well as that of others. In essence, one has the power to transform oneself and others from one pole to the other if one devotes the time and study necessary to master the art.

To destroy/eradicate out an undesirable rate of mental vibration... concentrate upon the opposite pole to that which you desire to suppress, changing the undesirable's polarity.
                                          ~ The Kybalion

Dr. King, Gandhi and Mother Teresa understood that in order to get to love and peace, one cannot engage in violence and war respectively.

In your household, if the engagement is back and forth in conflict, you will never get to peace. And, the possibility does exist that the conflict may escalate into violence.

Your greatest protection is not associated with guns, locks, bars, or alarm systems. Your greatest protection is in your alignment with Neter to strengthen and preserve your mental, physical, and emotional well-beings, which enhance your ability to hear and listen to Spirit in the guidance and purpose in your life. This is the Faith that you must have, the belief in the unseen.

The Netcheru is calling you to create a world enhancing and magnifying Life.

The accompanied companion to *Protection* and enriching your mental, physical and emotional well-beings is *Creation*. Through hearing and listening to Neter, Divine instruction, you are creating a world that protects and exalts life.

↔

Neter's word is pure. I will trust in it; it is my shield.

Neter's word is pure. I will trust in it; it is my shield.

Neter's word is pure. I will trust in it; it is my shield.

Next up: Household DNA's 4th Principle -
PROVISIONS

Breathe, I AM SPIRIT
Create, I AM LIGHT
Transform, I AM LOVE

Meditation / Quiet Time
Please take this moment to reflect on what you have
just read. Turn within.

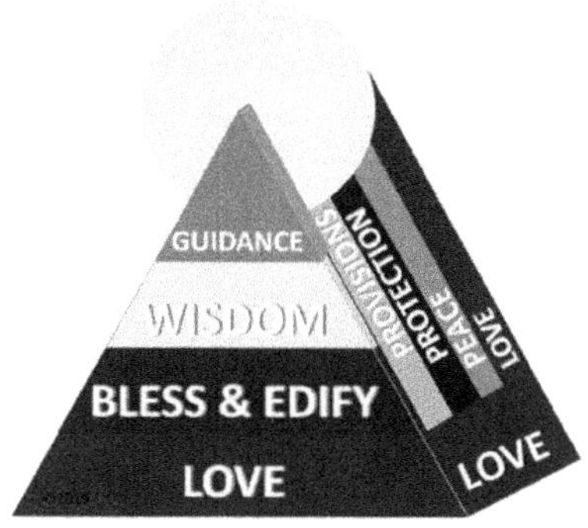

4th Essential Spiritual Principle of Self

Provisions

Behold the fowls of the air (Matthew 6:26): for they sow not, neither do they reap, nor gather into barns; yet your heavenly Father feedeth them. Are ye not much better than they?

↔

*The Fourth Principle of Household DNA is **Provisions**.*

The Lord is my Shepherd, I shall not want.

The Lord is my Shepherd, I shall not want.

The Lord is my Shepherd, I shall not want.

Psalm 23:
The LORD is my shepherd; I shall not want.
He maketh me to lie down in green pastures: he leadeth me beside the still waters.
He restoreth my soul: he leadeth me in the paths of righteousness for his name's sake.
Yea, though I walk through the valley of the shadow of death, I will fear no evil: for thou art with me; thy rod and thy staff they comfort me.
Thou preparest a table before me in the presence of mine ene-

mies: thou anointest my head with oil; my cup runneth over. Surely goodness and mercy shall follow me all the days of my life: and I will dwell in the house of the LORD forever.

Provisions – supply one's need, which makes one whole and enhances life and the understanding that one's life is worthy and is made in the image and likeness of Neter.

Let's repeat.

Provisions – supply one's need, which makes one whole and enhances life and the understanding that one's life is worthy and is made in the image and likeness of Neter.

Provisions functions as a support beam of the Household DNA Mir. Operating from Neter, brings you into the *Wholeness-Sustainment State of Being* where all provisions are delivered unto you.

The color associated with PROVISIONS on the Household DNA Mir is silver, which indicates that the *Power of Will* is needed for complete comprehension of the *Principle of Provisions.*

Will is the process of choosing one's purpose, determination and desires. Will is analogous to a compass. When *will* is set and focused in a certain direction, this is the direction of one's energy in their thoughts, words and actions.

> **The Heart is the Conscience and Will of Man, the Cause...**
> *~Understanding The Universal Law of Cause and Effect*
> *(Kemetic Teachings)*

When *the Heart* is set and focused in a certain direction, this is the direction of one's energy in their thoughts, words and actions.

The self, when guided by the ego and not the Spirit, has a *will* of its own. When the Self guides, there is not a consistent state of wholeness and sustainability.

However, when one moves to Spiritual guidance, *Divine Will* points the direction, leads, and chooses providing all one's needs, which makes one whole, enhances one's life and the understanding that one's life is worthy. Thus, one enters the *States of Beings of Wholeness and Sustainment.*

Therefore, it is time to educate, retrain, or reinforce our will in or-der to enter into or sustain the State where all our provisions are delivered – a state of being known as wholeness.

Let's learn.

The whole being is a sum of parts. The mind, body, soul, and the Spirit together make the whole being. Therefore, the whole being is only as strong as the weakest part. If any part is not whole, then the whole is not whole.

Neter is life not death, creation not destruction. Neter will not be in conflict with itself. Thus, the whole must enhance life and each individual part must maintain wholeness to contribute to the whole-being enhancing life. Additionally, the whole-being must show and represent the understanding that one is made in the image and likeness of Neter.

What you eat must enhance life; what you wear must enhance life; your shelter and your household must enhance life. Therefore, the provisions you choose must be life enhancing.

At this moment, ask yourself, how are you showing up in your life?

This is not about having more money to represent Divinity; this is about a decision to represent Neter and enhance life in your world.

The decision is yours to make. When you make a decision to listen to and follow Spirit, inherently you choose to allow Neter to provide for you. This is a relationship between *you and your Spirit.* And, when you make the choice to follow Spirit and allow Neter to provide for you, prepare for self-regulation when it comes to your wants.

Asking Spirit how and on what to spend Neter's money is guaranteed to give you an answer of *quality*, irrespective of quantity. This is *Glory to Glory to Glory with Neter* - the action of living in the Kingdom, Divine Consciousness.

Question:
How do you know you are hearing from Neter?

Here's the answer. Remember, Neter will not be in conflict with itself. If you are sensing anything on the opposite of Neter's pole: such as fear, weakness, and powerlessness…then, this is not *of Neter.* Therefore, this is not *with Neter.*

According to research, the Spirituality center is located in the right hemisphere of the brain. Because the right hemisphere of the brain controls the left side of the body, it is the belief that Spirit speaks to one in the left ear.

Real case scenario
Being one who hears from and listens to Spirit, I was amazed that the voice of Spirit does come through on my left side - my left ear.

Neter's polar end is power, love and a sound mind. Neter has not given us the Spirit of fear, but of power, love and a sound mind.

Please understand that your will, your desires, and your wants may or may not be of Neter. However, with *Divine Will* in Neter's provisions, there is no buyer's remorse, no need to return, no concern about how something will be received.

As you seek to fulfill your desires and wants, the key word is <u>*you*</u>.

Are you seeking or is Neter providing?

Where are you standing on the pole?

According to the *Universal Law of Polarity*, either you are standing on Neter's polar end seeking knowledge, wisdom, and guidance, or you are not.

Real case scenario
When Spirit led me to relocate, Spirit also led me into a life of minimalism. The wise use of Neter's resources resulted in a house, good health, peace of mind, travel, and more giving. Neter's guidance hasn't stressed me out, not one day, in 20+ years.

Faith grows through listening to Neter and seeing the results. In the summer of 2016, I was asked, "who do you work for?" The answer I gave was not of me but of the I AM within. I never shared or thought about the answer I provided. Who do you work for, I was asked. I stated with authority the answer, "I work for the KINGDOM." It was the most beautiful ah-ha moment in my world. I knew it came from the Supreme Being.

Your relationship with your Spirit will guide you on how and what to do with Neter's resources. Your relationship with your Spirit is a special relationship between you and Neter.

Unconditional love, happiness, sound mind, and power are just some of the experiences on Neter's end along with resurrection and restoration. Neter restoreth my soul.

On Neter's end, Neter's provisions make one whole. Neter's provisions are life exalting and radiate the image and likeness of Neter, a Divine Life-Force.

Understanding, seeking, and enhancing your relationship between you and Neter elevates your Spiritual awareness, living and deliverance to *Glory to Glory to Glory 'of Neter' which is quantity.* The quantity being throughout your life; surely goodness and mercy shall follow me all the days of my life, and I will dwell in the house of the LORD for ever. This is called Kingdom living.

Glory to Glory to Glory *'with Neter'* – *Quality*... Glory to Glory to Glory *'of Neter'* – *Quantity*...

↔

Provisions is a very unique principle of Household DNA because the fulfilling of wants and desires are based on what you go out, get, and ultimately decide to associate with and input into the body and the household. Up to this point, love, peace and protection were more about listening to and exhibiting Divinity from within to achieve these states of beings.

According to the *Universal Law of Cause and Effect*, there is no cause without effect and no effect without cause.

- Poor Quality food in results in poor quality health.
- The allowing of people who exhibit poor quality behavior in the home results in an increase in conflict in the household and sometimes violence.
- Toxicity allowed in the body and home results in toxicity in the body and household.

As stated earlier, as we increase our vibration, mentally rising in our thoughts, we understand our power as Causers, and not just being an effect. In this, *'We become the Masters of our Life'.*

Standing on Neter's end of the pole, listening to Spirit as it instructs one on how to use Neter's resources, yields the greatest quality of return, the greatest quality of mental, physical, and emotional well-being, and the greatest quality of life.

Your life is a story you help to author. Your life is an out picturing of your choices. Your life is for your choosing. Don't underestimate the power of choice, because your choices become your life. Your household is your wants and desires showing up in full effect.

Reinforce and retrain your *Will* to focus in the direction where all provisions are delivered, a direction towards Spirit allowing the ability of *Divine Will* to elevate you into a *State of Being known as Wholeness.*

The **Law of Life** as given to me by the Spirit and the Ancestors:

> *When your Human Consciousness elevates into your*
> *Divine Consciousness, when your Ego elevates into*
> *your Spirit, you will have elevated into the Kingdom.*
>
> (*When understanding the Law of Life, one will increase their vibration.*)
> ~*Queen Miata*

The accompanied companion to *Provisions* is *Patience*. Neter's provisions make one whole. When one is whole, one will exhibit a greater level of patience and Spiritual expression with others.

The Universe is calling you to experience and ascend into the Divine Consciousness, into the Kingdom living of Neter.

↔

The Lord is my Shepherd, I shall not want.

The Lord is my Shepherd, I shall not want.

The Lord is my Shepherd, I shall not want.

Next up: Household DNA's 5th Principle –
BLESS and EDIFY

Breathe, I AM SPIRIT
Create, I AM LIGHT
Transform, I AM LOVE

Meditation / Quiet Time
Please take this moment to reflect on what you have
just read. Turn within.

5th Essential Spiritual Principle of Self
Bless and Edify

*Bless and Edify align with the Kemetic Principle of
Medew Nefer, which means Good Speech.*

The Daily Nourishment Principles are located on the sides of the
Household DNA Mir. These principles (*Love*, *Bless and Edify*,
Wisdom and *Guidance*) feed and strengthen our soul and others.

As we are all individual parts of the *Universal Consciousness of
One*, we all play a role in the demonstration of Neter in the Universe and the Universe being balanced.

Each one of us is a vehicle, which through Spirit, Neter's goodness is expressed. The Soul is where the Spirit resides. The
Soul has to be fed and nourished properly, just like the mind and
body, to be open, receptive, and able to do Divine will.

*We interact daily with others of different levels of expressed
energy, from those walking in the greatest expression of
Divine light, to those walking in almost absolute darkness.*

Neter is love, and love is transformative power. Within each of
us, Neter's transformative power is the energy that moves others
out of darkness-death to Neter's light-life. It is through the daily

performance of these nourishing principles, we enlighten others.

↔

*The Fifth Principle of Household DNA is **Bless & Edify**.*

The Gift of Neter is life; I will Edify others; I will Speak life.

The Gift of Neter is life; I will Edify others; I will Speak life.

The Gift of Neter is life; I will Edify others; I will Speak life.

Simply put, in Psalm 19:14, *let the words of my mouth, and the meditation of my heart, be acceptable in thy sight.*

To Bless means to approve of, and to Edify means to enlighten. We pray for things of which we approve. When you Bless and Edify, you respond with good words and actions: you love in the words you speak, in the tone in which you speak, and in the actions you do.

Bless and Edify functions as a daily nourishment and behavior of the Household DNA principles. Therefore, we are to bless and edify daily. The practice of edification inherently means to bless.

The color associated with Bless and Edify on the Household DNA Mir is purple, which represents *Power*. Here, power is dispersed when you bless and edify.

Power is the ability to create. You have the power to create, and you have been creating your world based on your thoughts, your words, and your actions.

What we speak and what we do can be blessings or curses, life or death, edification or destruction. What we speak and do in love will bless and edify us and others, feeding, nourishing and strengthening the body, mind and soul.

With Neter being love, life, and light, it is very clear how Neter's power is to be used. In 2 Corinthians 13:10 it states, *according to the power which the Lord hath given me to edification, and not to destruction.*

Formerly mentioned were the 5 Divine Instructions given to me by Spirit during my initiation in my role as a Queen:

1) My default must be love.
2) Speak to everyone as if I am speaking to the Spiritual Father.
3) Never argue, debate, or try to convert.
4) Quickly get through my emotions and move forward.
5) Always lookup.

Number 2: *Speak to everyone as if I am speaking to the Spiritual Father* is Medew Nefer, Good speech.

With communication being 70%+ non-verbal, one can easily recognize how these Divine Instructions underscore the importance to Love, Bless and Edify. We are to use our Neter given power to create a world that enlightens self and others through the expression of love, life, and light.

↔

In a previous understanding on the *State of Being of Protection,* we referenced the energy associated with thoughts.

In my Physics class, I demonstrate this energy by elevating a pendulum in my hand and having it move, cycling to the left and then to the right. This is due to the thoughts in my mind generating nerve impulses in my brain that transport energy radiating through my arm, fingers, and the pendulum. The cycling of the pendulum is created by the cycling of Energy, caused by Earth's rotation due to gravitational pull, transferred to the pendulum.

When you think negative and hateful thoughts, there is energy associated with those thoughts being sent out into your world.

And, because energy is cycling, it affects others and rotates back around to you. You send out hate, hate comes back. You send out negative thoughts, and negativity comes back.

The unanswered question of sending out negative and hateful thoughts is you don't know how they will return. Because they affect others and you cannot control others, your thoughts can return as criticism or say for example, violence.

The same is true with hateful words and actions. In the book of Ephesian chapter 4 verse 29 it states, *let no corrupt communication proceed out of your mouth, but that which is good to the use of edifying, that it may minister grace unto the hearers.*

Words out of our mouth are supposed to be of *Good speech*; words are supposed to minister to others. According to the dictionary, minister means to give service, care, or aid; attend, as to wants or necessities… to contribute, as to comfort of happiness.

For example:
Young intelligent people, young intelligent young man, and young intelligent young lady are common words I use when addressing young people, teenagers.

Referencing Ephesians 4:16, when you engage in loving behavior, you edify all parts of the self, that's yourself. Therefore, your thoughts, words, and behavior not only edify others but they edify you. Your words and actions tell others how to interact with you and the quality of person you are. You are to use good words because words have power, and you create your world correspondingly.

> ***As within; so without. As without; so within.***
> *~The Universal Law of Correspondence,*
> *Kemetic Teaching (Mdu Ntr, Pert Em Heru)*

↔

Real case scenario
A young man entered my class and made reference to the N-word. I informed him that we don't use such words. He then stated, "We are all N's up in here." I gave him a task. I asked him to write down everything due him based on him referring to himself as a NIGGER or NIGGA; it really doesn't matter. Needless to say, his paper was blank.

Universal Laws keep the Universe balanced (*remember in* <u>*Chemistry*</u> *101 the need to balance equations, in Biotechnology, it's material balancing*). It is foolish to believe you can send something out, and it will not return. It will. According to the *Universal law of Cause and Effect*; there are consequences for our actions.

↔

Question:
What does your body inherently do everyday, minute, hour, and second?

Answer:
Your body tries to live. Inherently our body is hard-wired for life. If it wasn't, we would be dead. That's why one have to commit suicide.

The Universe and Earth are hard-wire to create and sustain life. If they weren't, we would be dead.

We are made in the image and likeness of the Netcheru, The Divine Universal Laws and Principles of Creation.

As above; so below. As below; so above.
~The Universal Law of Correspondence,
Kemetic Teaching (Mdu Ntr, Pert Em Heru)

↔

When you have negative thoughts, cancel them out with positive thoughts very quickly. When you speak negatively, quickly cancel the negative words by speaking positively. When you do something negative, quickly cancel it out by doing something positive; and, I do mean quickly. Don't let negativity take root.

Now, the practice of cancelling out negative thoughts, words, and actions should not be the norm for several reasons:

1) By the time you start engaging in the cancellation process, the effect may already have occurred.

The example that comes to mind is a man calling a woman a name and the woman responding with a SLAP. Harsh example, but you get the point.

2) The positive to negative ratio is about 7 to 1. It takes about 7 positives to cancel one negative, seven praises to cancel one criticism. Therefore, mathematically, this is nonsensical in a Universe that is quickening due to technological advances contributing to the expediency of consequences. (Just to note: The opposite is true; you can cancel several positive actions with one negative action.)

3) If you contribute to the permanent destruction of life, you can't undo the state of death.

4) You are creating a world of confusion, chaos, inconsistency, and instability by flip flopping between positive and negative actions.

James 3:10 puts it this way, *'Out of the same mouth proceedeth blessings and curses. My brethren, these things ought not so to be.'*

5) Lastly, you never deal with the cause…the why… Why are you having negative thoughts, saying negative words, and doing negative things?

The answer is in the true self-realization of knowing where you are standing on the pole between light and darkness,

Are you standing in the light, where Spiritual enlightenment is, listening to Neter, or are you standing in darkness, where Physical ignorance is, listening to self?

and where you are standing is based on your Heart, the location of one's conscience and will.

The Heart is the Conscience and Will of Man, the Cause, and the Tongue delivers what is in the Heart; thereby manifesting the Effect.
>   ~*Understanding The Universal Law of Cause and Effect*
>   *(Kemetic Teachings)*

Thoughts, Words, and Actions work to deliver what is in the Heart. Remember, words and actions follow thought. The real work of Bless and Edification comes from the Heart. The real work of transformation is to be done in the heart.

↔

Understand that embedded in the Universal system of balance is the concept of cycles. The cycles of seasons, years and days are based on the revolution of earth in conjunction with the sun and moon. This is the *Universal Law of Rhythm*: Ebb and Flow, Yin and Yang, Life and Death, etc.

According to the Kybalion, *"Everything flows, out and in...rise and fall...the measure of the swing to the right is the measure of the swing to the left; rhythm compensates...*

The *Law of Rhythm* states that energy in the Universe is like a pendulum. Whenever something swings to the right, it must then swing to the left. Everything in existence is involved in a dance: swaying, flowing, and swinging back and forth. Everything is either growing or dying. As everything and everyone is evolving and transforming, their evolution may not necessarily be towards Neter, listening to Neter, or expressing Neter.

Understanding the *Law of Rhythm* helps one to understand that the ups and downs, the mental highs and lows, come with and in life. When those negative swings come, you need to know how to get back to Neter, how to get back and stay in the Light, Divinity.

The Biblical number for transformation is 40. When an entity has existed in a practicing condition for 40 consecutive days, that entity has more or less transformed to that condition.

Thus, strengthening your relationship with Neter is very important. Through meditation, reading, and behavior, you feed, nourish, and strengthen your relationship with Neter increasing your ability to hear Neter's spirit and stay in Neter; stay in Spirit. In my practice, *Alignment of Consciousness,* I move my mind to align with the Divine Consciousness. I use the Divine Force within, Neter, to align with the Neter, the Divinity (the Creator); it is a very powerful high vibrational exercise.

Household members and others may be going through the negative swing of the pendulum. This is why our words and behavior must be love. Our words and behavior must bless and edify.

Due to the power that the Creator has given you, you can restore the souls of others. You can bless others. You can resurrect others from walking in darkness to walking in the light.

Psalm 34:1

I will bless the LORD at all times: his praise shall continually be in my mouth...

It is time to choose. Choose wisely. Life and death are in the power of the tongue. Therefore, choose life that both thou and thy seed may live.

We have the transformative power to resurrect, bless, and restore Household members from darkness to light. Don't underestimate your power; it was given to you by the Creator, Neter.

Move in your power, your Neter given dominion and transformative power.

The Universe is calling you to use your *Power* for the edification of others, moving and transforming others from death to life, from darkness to light.

The companion to *Bless and Edify* is *Life*. When you bless and edify, you enhance life.

↔

The Gift of Neter is life; I will Edify others; I will Speak life.

The Gift of Neter is life; I will Edify others; I will Speak life.

The Gift of Neter is life; I will Edify others; I will Speak life.

Next up: Household DNA's 6th Principle –
WISDOM

Breathe, I AM SPIRIT
Create, I AM LIGHT
Transform, I AM LOVE

Meditation / Quiet Time
Please take this moment to reflect on what you have
just read. Turn within.

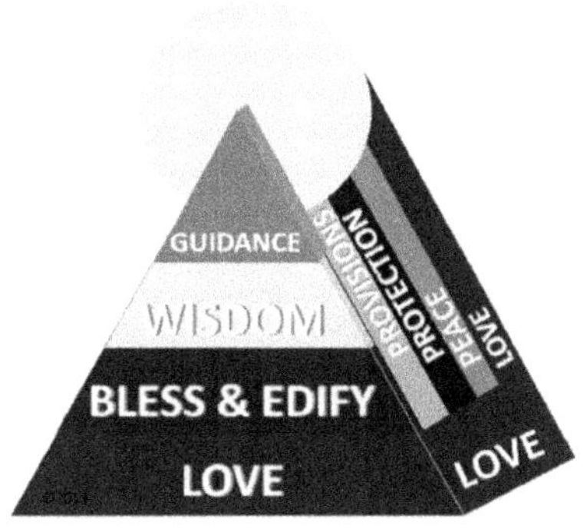

6th Essential Spiritual Principle of Self

Wisdom

Wisdom aligns with the Kemetic Principle of Medew Netcher, which means Divine Speech.

*The Sixth Principle of Household DNA is **Wisdom**.*

Neter giveth me Wisdom; my mouth shall speak of wisdom.

Neter giveth me Wisdom; my mouth shall speak of wisdom.

Neter giveth me Wisdom; my mouth shall speak of wisdom.

For the LORD giveth wisdom: out of his mouth cometh knowledge and understanding (Proverbs 2:6).

Wisdom – the ability to discern what is true, what causes the effect. One's mindset establishes the cause resulting in the effect. Seek knowledge and understanding, and teach to discern what is true, what is right.

Wisdom functions as a daily nourishment and behavior of the Household DNA principles. Therefore, we are to speak wisely, giving knowledge and understanding daily.

Speak from Neter, giving Spiritual Wisdom daily.

The color associated with Wisdom on the Household DNA Mir is yellow. Wisdom is one of the 12 powers of man, and it is represented by the color yellow.

Spiritual Wisdom is needed to feed others with wisdom. In essence, you have to have Divine wisdom to speak Divine speech.

When you speak Neter, you speak Wisdom.
When you speak Neter, you speak Understanding.
When you speak Neter, you speak Knowledge.

When you speak Neter, you speak Divine Speech.

And, there is no greater knowledge than the awareness of '*The Truth*'. The truth shall set you free, and there is no greater truth than you are made in the image and likeness of the Creator, the Divine Universal Principles and Laws of Creation, and the Divine Energy of Creation. From this truth, comes your wisdom, knowledge and understanding.

The true identity of all life is that all life is *Divine*. All life is '*of Neter*'. We are '*Divine and of Neter*'.

Light begets Light
Light begets Life

We are Spiritual Beings having a Human experience. Therefore, our thoughts, words, and actions must be '*of Spirit*'. 1 Corinthians 2:13 states, *"This is what we speak, not in words taught by human wisdom but in words taught by the Spirit, explaining Spiritual realties with Spirit-taught words."*

Real Case scenario
A parent called about her child's lack of motivation and progress. She wanted an in person consultation for what I registered as a quick resolution. I told her to have her household members write down 3 -5 words expressing their identity.

The son identified himself as a Young Black Man. I responded, 'that's your child's human identity. His first and true identity is 'of God'. I went on to explain the world's messaging for Black people is of limitations and negativity. Connecting him to his true identity imposes no such limitations. Thoughts, words, and actions in the household changed, and there was no additional consultation needed.

Connecting to your true identity being Neter imposes no limitations. Elevate into the understanding that you are of Neter.

Human Beings have been categorized and conditioned out of their true identity. They commonly and humanly refer to themselves as White, Black, Male, Female, etc. Subsequently, creating separation from the Divine and limits based on their human ignorance.

My daughter once asked, at a very very early age, aren't we African Americans? I told her that is a human identity. Human identities change. First we were Colored, Black, now African Americans. However, your true identity never changes; you are 'of God'. And, you selected the particular Human vehicle because of the <u>amazing</u> impact it will make as you express your Divine purpose.

One note - Identification boxes were never a problem because there was always the knowledge, understanding, and wisdom that these are human games that human beings play. We are Spiritual beings in a human world filled with people who know not who they are and know not what they do.

You are 'of Neter'...Pure Love, Pure Energy, Divinely created in the image and likeness of Neteru. Your body only allows you to have a Human experience to express the Greatness of Neter in your world, which occurs when you adhere to Spiritual guidance, and let *Divine Will* lead.

According to the *Universal Law of Correspondence*, when you know thyself, you will know everything that is around you and in the universe because there is harmony, agreement, and correspondence between the physical, mental, and spiritual realms.

As above; so below. As below; so above.
~*Kemetic Teaching (Mdu Ntr, Pert Em Heru)*

↔

Imagine the Capital Letter 'L'. Neteru/God is at the top of the L, top of the vertical component. You are located where the two lines meet, and the other end of the lower horizontal line outreaches to your world.

'L' is the symbol of our connection to the Creator. If you want to know why something is showing up in your life, simply check what you think, what you say, and what you do. Be honest.

Are you thinking out of your Greatness, the Neter of you?

Are you speaking out of your Greatness, the Neter of you?

Are you doing out of your Greatness, the Neter of you?

Your world is a mirror image of your connection to Neter or the lack thereof. Notice how the word Neter is used to discuss the Supreme Being. Different words may be used; however, use a term that represents all power, all knowledge, and all presence. Some will use Netcheru, God, Universe, others Divinity, and others will use the term One.

In high esteem, the truth is in the knowledge that we are all connected. We are all connected to a Universal Consciousness reference here as *The Universal Consciousness of One*. The Spirit of Netcheru all around us is the Spirit of Netcher in each one of us. And, the Spirit of Netcher in each one of us is a part of the Spirit of Netcheru all around us.

There are three areas of Spiritual Enlightenment of which you must have understanding.

The first area of Spiritual enlightenment is the Universal laws.

I. The Universal Laws

Wisdom is in the knowledge and understanding that our one connection to the Universal mind means we are all affected by what each one does independently and any of us collectively. Hence, we are all affected by Universal laws, whether you know it, believe it or not.

My Spiritual enlightenment exponentially has elevated since studying and practicing the Seven Ancient African Universal Laws. I had previously heard of the Laws of Attraction and Consequences, but there was never an *ah-ha* moment of Spirit saying to me, the Scientist and Metaphysicist, pay attention and learn this. That moment came when I was introduced to the Kybalion, I was like a child in a candy store, studying every word, learning, and engaging in thought-provoking discussions. This made sense because my 2nd Spirit-led book, *'God has not forgotten you'*, contextually referenced and illuminated all 7 Ancient African Universal Laws without their titles.

Shortly afterward, Spirit gave me my instructions: enlighten the world with this knowledge in the task I have given you; the task being the explanations of the 7 Spiritual Principles of Self, Household DNA.

Please understand, the 7 Spiritual Principles of Self / Household DNA principles and their presentation using the Mir were given to me and created in 2013. We tried to deliver its full understanding in 2014. Spirit shut the project down. The task was set to the side until February 2016 when I was told of my task.

Approximately 40 days later, during the first week of April 2016, I was introduced to the 7 Ancient African Universal Laws. In May 2016, Spirit spoke to me in New York when Spirit wrote *Your Greatest Potential* through me, and the writings of the 7 Spiritual Principles of Household DNA detailed explanation began its manifestation.

It is an honor to serve as Spirit unleashes a powerful kept knowledge to its people. As I am led by Spirit, I continue to learn the knowledge, understanding, and wisdom of our Ancestors. It is imperative to understand history for self-awareness and self-actuality in *Living in Your Light.*

↔

You have been exposed to them. Now, here is the list of the Seven Alkebu-Lan (Africa) Universal Laws for your further study and acquisition of wisdom.

Seven Ancient African Universal Laws
I. The Universal Law of MENTALISM.
II. The Universal Law of CORRESPONDENCE.
III. The Universal Law of VIBRATION.
IV. The Universal Law of POLARITY.
V. The Universal Law of RHYTHM.
VI. The Universal Law of CAUSE AND EFFECT.
VII. The Universal Law of GENDER

Neter giveth wisdom; therefore, seek the knowledge of understanding of it.

Who is a wise person?

According to Proverbs 18:15, *it is one who getteth knowledge.*

↔

The second area of Spiritual enlightenment is the 12 Powers of Man.

II. The 12 Powers of Man

The numbers 7 and 12 are numbers of completion. The 12 Powerer of Man are Spiritual Gifts. In my study of the 12 Powers of Man, I do find difference in the body location given for some of the Powers. For example, the location of Will is given in the mind. When I followed the Light within, the Divine Force, it took me back to the undiluted Power of Spirituality in Alkebu-Lan (Ancient Africa), and I learned and understood the truth. The true location of Will is in the Heart.

These 12 powers are to be use under the influence of *Spiritual guidance*. If you use them from the understanding of self-guidance Human wisdom, they will eventually lead to death, which is demonstrated by a State of Being of Stagnation, represented by the inability to create, grow, and enhance life.

Twelve Powers of Man:

<u>Divine Faith</u>
Let's look at Faith. Miracles are nothing but manifestations of Divine Faith...*There is no Human plan for the outcome*. However, at the self-end of the pole, you plan, you work and eventually you manifest an outcome, like purchasing a product. Was this really Divine Faith? Absolutely not! Why? Well, you already knew you were going to have the funds to purchase the product.

Divine Faith is when you move through an unseen step-less plan based on Spiritual Guidance.

<u>Divine Love</u>
Now, let's look at Divine Love. We discussed the emotional Loves, one minute you love them and the next minute you don't.

Divine Love is Agape Love, Spirit generated and unconditional.

Divine Power

Human power is to control someone having them to submit. How long do you think that will last? However, *Divine Power* is one of creating your world and enhancing life.

Divine Imagination

Imagination means to image and envision basically anything positive and negative. However, *Divine Imagination* is from the standpoint of Neter. Therefore, the images are good and enhance life; they picture the Goodness of life being envisioned in your mind creating your world expressing Neter. *Divine imagination* inherently understands that images are thoughts, which we move through and manifest.

Divine Order

Human order may be one of protocols and steps. However, *Divine order* includes balance and harmony. Divine order will not lead you into unresolvable conflict and imbalance.

Divine Elimination

What about Elimination…removal of junk and waste from the Human self-perspective. However, *Divine Elimination* is one of renunciation, forgiveness, and transformation.

The others: **Divine Will, Divine Life, Divine Zeal, Divine Strength, Divine Understanding, and Divine Wisdom**, have been or will be referenced in detail.

↔

The third area of Spiritual enlightenment is the Power of love.

III. The Power of Love

The *greatest* of these powers is Love – Divine Love, Agape

Love. Agape Love is benevolence, kindness, devotion, and goodwill.

When the Heart is locked up in resistance (despair, trauma, unforgiveness), the Spirit is not free. Agape love is the key to unlocking and elevating the heart, freeing the Spirit. The Spirit takes flight ascending one to the Light. The Divine Force within you is your Light. One must operate from the Divine Force within to Live.

A new commandment I give to you (John 13:34), *that you love one another; as I have loved you, that you also love one another.* This is the Golden Rule.

The Golden rule is expressed in many religions and represents the **Universal Consciousness of One** giving rise to our **Unity**.

In Christianity the proclamation is: Do unto others what you would have them do unto you; this sums up the Law of the Prophets…

Hinduism reads: This is the sum of duty: do naught unto others which would cause you pain if done to you.

Buddhism states: Hurt not others in ways that you yourself would find hurtful.

Islam recites: No one of you is a believer until he desires for his brother that which he desires for himself.

Judaism professes: What is hateful to you do not to your fellow man. This is the entire Law; all the rest is commentary.

Bahai Faith confesses: And if thine eyes be turned towards justice, choose thou for thy neighbor that which thou choosest for thyself.

The fourth area of Spiritual enlightenment is the 7 Spiritual Principles of Self / Household DNA.

IV. The 7 Spiritual Principles of Self / Household DNA

1. Agape Love
2. Peace
3. Protection
4. Provisions
5. Bless and Edify
6. Wisdom
7. Guidance

↔

This is Project 'L'. 'L' represents your connection with Neter being connected to what is showing up in Household and in your World. Project 'L' is rooted in the Divine wisdom that the love, life, and light in your world is your relationship to the Supreme Being you are allowing to be expressed.

The wisdom that we must feed others with daily is the truth, which never changes. Operating from Neter, Spiritual Guidance, we feed self and others with Divine Speech.

There are Seven components of the Truth:

1) The truth being, we are made in the image and likeness of Divinity. Therefore, our identity is Divine. We are Spiritual Beings having a Human experience.

2) The truth being, Divine Love, Light, and Living come from listening to Spirit and allowing Neter's goodness to be expressed through us making us whole.

3) The truth being, Your Divine plan and purpose will only manifest through following Neter from the Spirit within you.

4) The truth being, we are all affected by the 7 Universal Laws whether we know them, believe them, accept them, or not.

5) The truth being, you were given 12 powerful gifts to be used under Spiritual Guidance for the edification of self and others; and, to grow, create, and exalt Life.

6) The truth being, the Greatest gift is the Power of Love, Agape Love, because Love transforms.

7) The truth being we are all connected. We are all connected to a Universal Consciousness. What one does independently or any collectively affects us all. We are all individual parts of the *Universal Consciousness of One*.

Wise people know there is no such thing as undemonstrated understanding. One acts according to their level of understanding, period. Wise people also know that they are here as an expression of Divinity – Neter.

Finally, wise people must remember to be wise.

The Universe is calling you speak Wisdom.

The companion to *Wisdom* is *Restoration and Resurrection of the Soul*.

↔

Neter Giveth me Wisdom. My mouth shall speak of wisdom.

Neter Giveth me Wisdom. My mouth shall speak of wisdom.

Neter Giveth me Wisdom. My mouth shall speak of wisdom.

Next up: Household DNA's 7th Principle -
GUIDANCE

Breathe, I AM SPIRIT
Create, I AM LIGHT
Transform, I AM LOVE

Meditation / Quiet Time
Please take this moment to reflect on what you have
just read. Turn within.

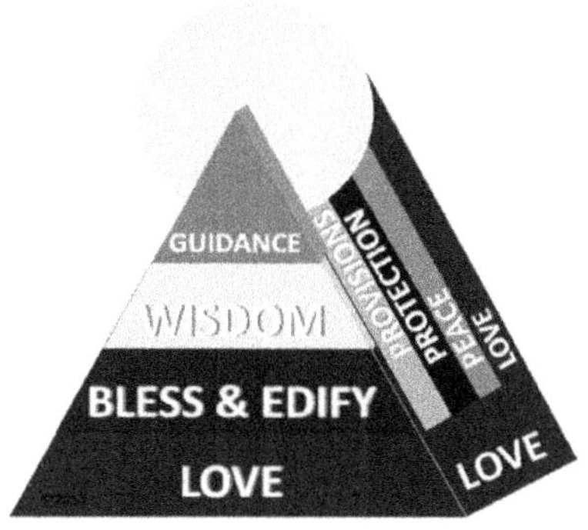

7th Essential Spiritual Principle of Self

Guidance

Guidance aligns with the Kemetic Principle of Weheme Mesu - Repetition of the Rebirths.

*The Seventh Principle of Household DNA is **Guidance.***

Neter will guide me in all truth; I am the light of the world.

Neter will guide me in all truth; I am the light of the world.

Neter will guide me in all truth; I am the light of the world.

Let your light so shine before men, that they may see your good works, and glorify your Father which is in heaven, Matthew 5:16.

The seventh and last Principle of Household DNA is Guidance – direct, manage, show, and lead one's energy towards its purpose. Guide through the understanding that one creates their world and destiny based on thoughts, words, and behavior bringing these things into visible manifestation.

Guidance functions as a daily nourishment and behavior of the Household DNA principles. Therefore, we must guide from and through Neter daily.

The color associated with Guidance on the Household DNA Mir is light green, which represents the *Power of Strength*. Here, Spiritual strength is needed for the complete understanding of Spiritual guidance to self and others. Spiritual strength includes the ability to endure and stay on course, especially, the staying on course part.

You guide from and through Spiritual guidance. You guide by delivering the truth in your thoughts, words and actions.

The truth never changes. There are seven components of the truth:

1) The truth being, we are made in the image and likeness of Neteru. Therefore, our identity is '*of Neter*'. We are Spiritual Beings having a Human experience.

2) The truth being, Divine Love, Light, and Living comes from listening to Spirit and allowing Neter's goodness to be expressed through us making us whole.

3) That truth being, Your Divine plan and purpose will only manifest through following Spiritual guidance from the Neter within you.

4) The truth being, we are all affected by the 7 Universal Laws whether we know them, believe them, accept them or not.

5) The truth being, you were given 12 powerful gifts to be used under Spiritual guidance for the edification of self and others; and, to grow, create, and exalt Life.

6) The truth being, the *greatest* gift is the Power of Love, Agape love, because Love transforms.

7) The truth being, we are all connected. We are all connected to a Universal Consciousness. What one does independently or any collectively affects us all. We are all individual parts of the *Universal Consciousness of One*.

Again, **y**ou guide from and through Spiritual guidance. You guide by delivering the truths in your thoughts, words and actions.

The truth never changes.

Luke 1:79 states, *"Give light to them that sit in darkness and in the shadow of death, to guide our feet into the way of peace."*

This is very important. It is very difficult for a person who is not in peace to hear Neter. We spoke of this earlier in the discussion of the *Principle of Protection*.

What is Darkness?
Darkness is the absence of light.

The *State of Being in Darkness* is the existence of being in the absence of Neter in the above stated truths.

Real case Scenario
Although I listen to and follow Spirit, I was in darkness in reference to knowing and understanding the 7 Ancient African Universal Laws. My Guide was a person whom my Spirit has named 'The Spirit of Joseph'. The Neter in him helped to unblock my Spirit, which was limited due to residual despair (resistance I thought was cleared) caused by a Divorce .

What is light?
Light is Energy.

And, the *State of Being in Light* is the existence of being in the presence of Neter, Pure Energy – all powerful, all present, all knowing.

You must understand what occurred upon your birth into the world. You took your first breath and entered the Earth plane in your physical body, into your self. Unfortunately, many of us, not all 100% of us, but most forgot our connection to the Spiritual realm.

We entered self, and without the proper Guide in our lives, we live and oscillate back and forth between the States of Beings in light and darkness. In self and being born in self or a state of darkness, we have forgotten our Spiritual connection to the Divine. This is not a punishment. You did absolutely nothing wrong.

However, here is what many of us have heard, '*you were born in sin*'. Imagine hearing those words as a child over and over and over again; you were born in sin. 'You were born in sin'; for many have heard this every Sunday, year after year, conditioning them to believe: they are bad, leading them to believe their conception was not ordained by Divinity, not warranted, or parents were sinful in their conception and birth.

Listen to the following 3 definitions of the word SIN according to dictionary:

1. Sin: transgression of divine law: *the sin of Adam.*

2. Sin: any act regarded as such a transgression, especially a willful or deliberate violation of some religious or moral principle.

3. SIN: any reprehensible or regrettable action, behavior, lapse, etc.; great fault or offense

Here are some truths: You did none of these things upon your birth; You committed no sin, and your birth was not sinful; Your birth was acknowledged by the Creator; You are of Divine Creation, and Neter loves you.

Let's shine the light of the Creator's truth on your birth. In the Spiritual realm, you put a plan in motion of your life on Earth. The plan included a purpose.   To significantly understand this, you must fully understand incarnation - a topic deserving more time than this platform allows. However, it is a common belief that we come with a Divine Purpose and a Divine Plan.

Continuing, we were born in *self,* comprised of a body, soul, and mind. And, in our *soul* is Spirit, the connection to the Supreme Being known as Neter. Being born in self, nearly all of us forget our Spiritual connection to Neter. We passed through the birth canal entering into a state of darkness, forgetting and not being aware of our Spiritual Connection.

In the state of darkness, we continue to exist and operate in self. We inflict nonsense and untruths into our world, in our thoughts, in the words we speak, and in our actions, using our power and energy creating a world contradicting life – a world of negativity and disorder.   This is called 'Self-Induced Nonsense' (S.I.N.); get it - Self-Induced Nonsense, S.I.N.

Self –induced nonsense develops early on out of our forgetfulness of our Spiritual connection to Divinity. If our parents never remember their connection to the Divine, then self-induced nonsense is taught. Later in our life, self-induced nonsense is probably contributed more to our choosing.

However, the rod of correction is tangible, which means to simply align with what is true – Neter, God, Spirit, Universe, Oneness, Divine Consciousness, whatever you call it. If we have forgotten, then we can remember. If we have chosen to stay disconnected from Neter, we can choose to connect with Neter.

The light of Neter surrounds us is being expressed in various forms of life-giving direction to acknowledge Neter and turn within.

Whatever your purpose is, trust Neter and with Neter, it is doable, and it is Great. In addition, the vehicle and conditions you have selected for your human experience are because of the amazing impact they will make as you express your Divine purpose.

When Human beings choose to operate in truth as Spiritual beings, they light their world. They let their light shine as Guides to others. You will know these Spiritual beings because their words and actions will be for you to follow and listen to the Spirit within you, and they will speak truths. They will not speak of themselves as the Divine, they will not try to replace the Divine in your life, and they will not ask you to follow them. Spiritual Beings of the light will focus you on turning within to the Spirit of Neter for guidance.

Additionally, they will speak truths.

Please understand, your Divine plan and your purpose are your Divine plan and your purpose. Others cannot tell you what your Divine plan and purpose are. Therefore, the message for the following of your Divine plan and purpose is within you and you only. Your Spirit is the ultimate Guide in facilitating the completion of your Divine plan and finding and living your Divine purpose.

The ability of Humans to operate as Spiritual Beings exists in all of us. However, choosing to operate may be hindered by our relationships with others, traditions, habits, rituals, or DNA, which delivers emotional memory during your initial creation and the processes of mitosis and meiosis. So, for many we go back and forth, to and fro, with our connection with Neter, which causes the switching of our light on and off.

Parents, ministers, family, friends may all serve as Guides when they are reinforcing you to turn within to the Spirit of Neter and obey only the Spirit of Neter, not them. However, I have found that many do not understand the why and how of the *Power of Agape love.* When the Spirit is locked in despair, one is unable to connect to the Light. Despair, trauma, and unforgiveness act as resistors to the flow of Energy in the body. It is Agape love the frees the Spirit allowing Energy to flow from one's self.

Real Case Scenario
My father was a minister. When he made his transition, he was over 80 years old. He read constantly. Over the years, I was a witness to his growth and elevation in Spiritual Understanding and Enlightenment. I asked him, why we do attend Church. He stated, to fellowship with others.

As for the relationship between parents and children, parents are selected conduits. Children come through you, but they are not yours, they are *of the Creator, Neter.*   When you choose to be a parent, you have inherently chosen to be a guide, a light in your child's life. Your thoughts, words, and behaviors are to be strengthened and aligned with the Neter within you.

The rod of correction is the teaching of correct behavior opposite the incorrect behavior.

You shall teach them diligently to your children [impressing God's precepts on their minds and penetrating their hearts with His truths] and shall speak of them when you sit in your house and when you walk on the road and when you lie down and when you get up.

- Deuteronomy 6:7 AMP

To teach diligently is training your child in connecting with Spirit for guidance. Teaching a child to honor people, means teaching them to recognize what people have done and guides the child in discerning what is good (of Divinity, Neter) and what is not 'of Good' (of Ego, Self). What is good can be imitated, what isn't good can be discarded. Guide a child from the position of honoring not raising from a position of obeying.

Train up a child in the way he should go: and when he is old, he will not depart from it.
- Proverbs 22:6.

As a guide, you will be fed instructions by Neter as you turn within. Many engage in meditation and quiet time to receive instruction from the Spirit of Neter within. As I mentioned before, I use a very powerful practice of Neter developed through the Spirit in I (SI) called *Alignment of Consciousness.*

Human wisdom is not Divine wisdom. As a Guide, you operate through and from Spiritual guidance. This is the strength that you must have, the strength to stay focus and on course operating from Neter, Spiritual wisdom, as you light your world.

Again, you guide from and through Neter, Spiritual Guidance. You guide by delivering the truths in your thoughts, words and actions.

Hosea Williams stated, *"I never met God until I met Martin Luther King Jr. King was not my God, but the true God was revealed to me through King."*

Dr. Martin Luther King was an awesome Guide.

The Harvest is plentiful my brothers and sisters, Matthew 9:37, *but the workers are few.*

The Universe is calling you to light the world.

Ye are the light of the world. A city that is set on a hill cannot be hid, Matthew 5:14.

The companion to *Guidance* is the expression of *Neter's Goodness: wholeness, oneness and love.*

↔

Neter will guide me in all truth; I am the light of the world.

Neter will guide me in all truth; I am the light of the world.

Neter will guide me in all truth; I am the light of the world.

This is Permission to be Great: *Love, Life, and Light.*

"The possession of Knowledge, unless accompanied by a manifestation and expression in Action, is like the hoarding of precious metals–a vain and foolish thing. Knowledge, like Wealth, is intended for Use. The Law of Use is Universal, and he who violates it suffers by reason of his conflict with natural forces. "
~the Kybalion

Next up:
I AM SPIRIT

Breathe, I AM SPIRIT
Create, I AM LIGHT
Transform, I AM LOVE

Meditation / Quiet Time
Please take this moment to reflect on what you have
just read. Turn within.

Live In Your Greatness
Part III– Epilogue

Your 'I AM SPIRIT'

SOUL and ENERGY

Breathe, **I AM SPIRIT**. Spirit comes form the word Spirae or some will say Spir. Both mean to breathe (i.e. respiration is the act of breathing).

When a newborn baby comes into existence, they have to breathe in to live. The newborn has to breathe in the *Breath of Life*; they have to breathe in the *Spirit of Life*.

However, when you go way back thousands and thousands and thousands and many thousands of years ago in Alkebu-Lan (Africa), our Ancestors used a term aligned with the *Energy of Life*. They used the term **Soul**. The *Soul of Life* takes into account the *Energy of Life*.

Therefore, when you engage in the act of breathing, you engage in breathing in the *Energy of Life*, the *Soul of Life*. You are engaging in the actions involved in creating and sustaining life.

When life is created, inherent in life is Kinetic energy. In James Weldon Johnson's poem 'The Creation' it reads:

> *...God scooped the clay...Till He shaped*
> *it in his own image; Then into it He blew*
> *the breath of life. And man became a*
> *living soul.*

Thus, one must not only look at what Spirit is, one must look at what Spirit does. In understanding the Universe, this Divine Universe, this creation, and how one came into creation, one must understand the Energy of Life, the Soul. It is this Soul that gives one Life.

Remember, energy is the ability to do work, and in order to do work, you have to have a force. In order to do work, you have to push and/or pull on the entities within the Universe to create.

To have the truest understanding of the term, **I AM SPIRIT** in creation one must understand the terms soul and energy. With Soul being life and Energy being a force, when you understand the Soul and the Energy, you understand the **Life-Force**. *In essence, when you are breathing in, you are breathing in the Life-force, the force of Energy that gives life.*

Inherent in the Soul is the connection to the Divine Universe, a connection to understanding the creations of the Creator. The creations of the creator have a Life-force that can produce, sustain, and maintain life. This is very powerful!

When we come into the Dimension of Life, inherent in us is the ability to engage in the process of producing life.

I AM SPIRIT is a common term for the common action of breathing. However, when you look at the root, the origin of its meaning, it reinforces the understanding of a force in the Universe that is so powerful that it produces life; you have that power.

Our Ancestors used the term NETER (NTR) to reference this powerful Life-force. Neter means the Divine Force within. The Divine force within us, Neter, connects us to the Divine Creator, and we are the Creator's creation. In all things that the Creator creates, there is Neter, the Divine force within. A Divine force that engages in the process of producing life. You are of Neter.

The Earth, the Sky, the Waters, the Sun, the Moon, Us, etcetera, all engage in the process of producing and sustaining life.

I AM SPIRIT. I AM the Soul of Life. I AM the Energy of Life. And, as the Energy of Life, as the Creator's creation, I also have the ability to engage in the process of creation to create.

When a baby breathe in Spirit, the baby's body and all the functions needed for life kicks into action. The body, the organs, the cells, and everything that needs to be done for life lines up and do what needs to be done.

A Life-force is Soul and Energy, Energy and the Soul, the Soul of Life. In order to have power, you have to have a force. It is this force, the Life -force that give us Life so we can stand and say **I AM SPIRIT.**

↔

The Proclamation
You are '*of Neter*' You are '*of Spirit*', and your name is **'I AM'**.

You have been living this Spiritual power everyday of your life whether you have known it, believed it or not.

You have been creating your world, bringing thoughts, words, and actions into visible manifestation based on what is in the blank following your 'I AM ___________' statement.

Recklessly filling in the blank with degrading, hateful, and victimizing terms created the chaos you live. Many have not known the cause of their world that shows up in full effect. Now you know.

Thoughts, words, and actions are supposed to edify. However, the recklessness of our words has kept many of us in this perpetual state of chaos, powerlessness and hate.

My ignorance of 'Who I AM' causes me to use my power for self–destruction.

Our design is amazing. I remember watching '*Roots*'. I remember asking my mother about women being raped. She stated, "They can take your body, but you have to give your mind."

Here's the truth, one can touch your physical body, we have to give up our mental self, but our Spiritual being is not ours to give. This is the center from which our resurrection occurs.

↔

Today, we stop and turn the other cheek. We turn to our Spiritual side to guide and fill in the blank of the 'I AM' statement.

We turn to the *Greatest* of us, the *Greatness* in us.

I AM SPIRIT and as SPIRIT:
I AM choosing to think from the *Greatest* of me, the *Greatness* in me, the '*Neter*' of me.

I AM SPIRIT and as SPIRIT:
I AM choosing to speak from the *Greatest* of me, the *Greatness* in me, the '*Neter*' of me.

I AM SPIRIT and as SPIRIT:
I AM choosing to act from the *Greatest* of me, the *Greatness* in me, the *'Neter'* of me.

`I Operate from the Supreme of me, NETER, the GOOD, the MAGNIFICIENT.

This is Permission to be Great!

There is a Supreme of me, within, consisting of Magnificent Creative Energy and Power. It is mines to access; it is my *greatest* potential; it is my transformative power to use and to elevate me and my household to *Greatness*.

↔

I will operate from the Supreme of me.

I will operate from the Supreme of me.

I will operate from the Supreme of me.

This is my Project L.
Operating in my Love, Life and Light.
Operating in my Greatness.
*Operating in my **I AM SPIRIT**.*

The End.

Breathe, I AM SPIRIT
Create, I AM LIGHT
Transform, I AM LOVE

You have *PERMISSION TO BE GREAT*!

Now, GO BE GREAT!

My Declaration

I AM A SPIRITUAL BEING

**I will live in my Greatness.
I will light up my world with the
Netcheru expression of the Netcher
within me of Divine Will.**

Poem

ENLIGHTENMENT

by Queen Miata

(In 2018, Spirit wrote these words in my mind just before the Spring Equinox.)

ENLIGHTENMENT
...by Queen Miata

Someone who turns back the hands of time
Born in darkness, but is able to climb

Someone who turns back the hands of time
Learns to walk, but is able to fly

Someone who turns back the hands of time
Lives in a nest, but never is able to rest

Someone who turns back the hands of time
Moves slow, but is able to go

Someone who turns back the hands of time
Passes through Mother Earth's second womb
Taking flight with Eagle's wings ascends to the light

Someone who turns back the hands of time
Becomes a star and guides

Someone who turns back the hands of time
LIVES!

The assignment as Queen Miata manifested itself in 2018 when Spirit told me to create a Nation enlightened in the Universal Laws, a nation who understands moving in the temerity of the Divine Force, the Creator's Energy, within.

I acknowledge and understand my Ascension.

~ Queen Phyllis L-Miata

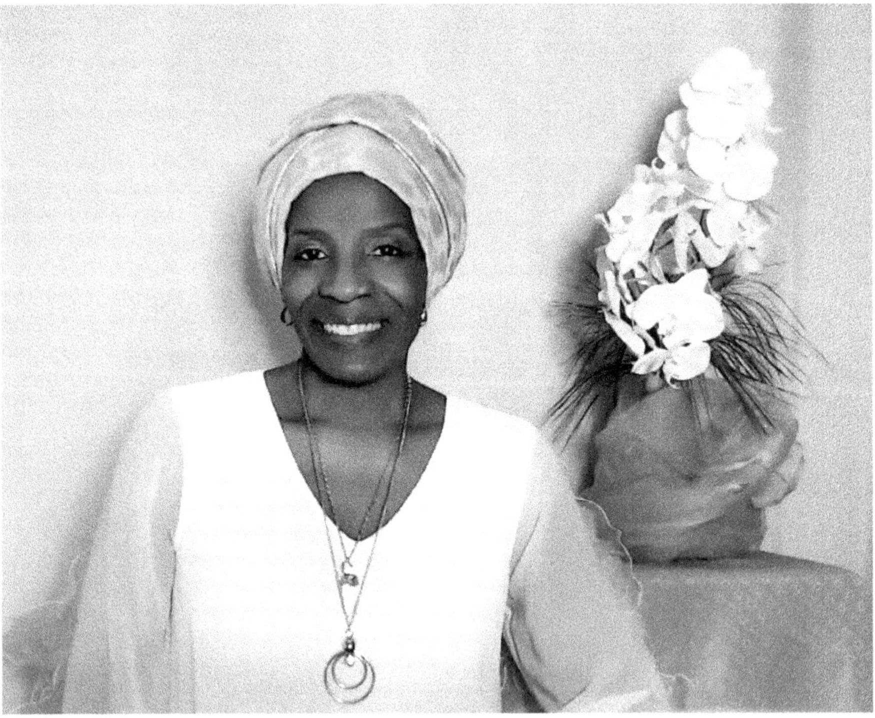

**It is time for a Rebirth.
It is time for Weheme Mesu.**

~Queen Miata

SPIRITUAL BEINGS, **RISE**!
SPIRITUAL BEINGS, **ASCEND**!
SPIRITUAL BEINGS, **LIVE**!

You have Permission to Be Great!

Breathe, *I AM SPIRIT*
Create, *I AM LIGHT*
Transform, *I AM LOVE*

Works by Queen Phyllis L-Miata:
www.PhyllisL-Miata.com
www.OneNationEnlightened.net

BOOKS:
Available for purchase online.

Permission To Be Great
Rise and Live in your Greatness

From Parent to Power
Written for Parents, Guardians, and Caretakers

God Has Not Forgotten You
Written for ages 14 – 24, but what everyone should know.

Workbook: *God Has Not Forgotten You*
Engages the reader of the book: *God Has Not Forgotten You* to think, create, and write about their destiny. Puts the reader on the road to transforming their life.

↔

VIDEOS:
Available for viewing on-demand online.

Weheme Mesu - REBIRTH: The Series
Before the Rebirth, the Season of Rest, Preparation and Renewal

7 Teachings in the Kingdom
Lessons of THE UNIVERSAL LAWS to Elevate Your Vibration

Reconciliation Series
Harmonizing Your Light As Nature Intended

In The Kingdom, I Am Kingdom
Ascension and Ascending 4 part series - Summer Solstice 2020

Additional podcasts, blogs, reading material, videos, etc. are available online. O.N.E. Global Kingdom is Your Kingdom to Grow, to Study, to be Enlightened, and to Elevate into Your Spiritual Power.

There is a Supreme of You within,
consisting of Magnificent Creative Energy and Power . . .

Permission
TO BE GREAT

Your Greatest Potential, Your Household DNA, Your 'I AM SPIRIT'

Queen Phyllis L-Miata, M.Ed.

www.PhyllisL-Miata.com